The Rosary

Mysteries of Joy, Light, Sorrow and Glory

Alice Camille

Drawings by Mary Southard, CSJ

ACTA

ASSISTING CHRISTIANS TO ACT

PUBLICATIONS

The Rosary: Mysteries of Joy, Light, Sorrow and Glory
by Alice Camille
with drawings by Mary Southard, CSJ

Edited by Kass Dotterweich
Cover design by Tom A. Wright
Typesetting by Desktop Edit Shop, Inc.

Scripture quotes are based on the author's compiled reflections from various translations.

Published by: ACTA Publications
            Assisting Christians To Act
            4848 N. Clark Street
            Chicago, IL 60640-4711
            773-271-1030

Library of Congress Catalog Number: 2003104386
ISBN: 0-87946-246-9
Printed in the United States of America
Year: 10 09 07 06 05 04 03
Printing: 10 9 8 7 6 5 4 3 2 1

Contents

Dedication

For Constance Ann Sophy, RSM,
Sister of Mercy,
friend in need,
mirror of the love of God

Introduction

Our Journey with the Rosary

Even my youngest siblings, born after 1960, do not quite remember when the Catholic world was first and foremost a "Marian" culture. For example, the building that housed our grade school was known as "M.O.C.," which stood for Mother of Consolation. The church the bishop employed when he came to town was Our Lady of Mount Carmel. Around the diocese one could readily find churches named after and dedicated to Mary: the Church of the Assumption, the Immaculate Conception, Queen of Peace, Notre Dame, St. Mary's, as well as Old St. Mary's. The local Catholic high school was Our Lady of Lourdes. Five girls in my class were named Mary, and many others had double names, like Mary Alice, Ann Marie, Margaret Mary, and Mary Catherine.

People wore the Miraculous Medal back then, with Mary's coat of arms emblazoned on the back. Some even kept the scapular handy, with Saint Simon Stock kneeling before Mary pictured on one side and the affirmation for a happy death printed on the other. In honor of Mary, we attended Mass on Saturdays, not to mention on her many feasts, sometimes because attendance was obligatory and sometimes for fervor's sake. And there were two whole months of the year given over to Mary: May and October. It was the sort of world in which it made perfect sense when I was a teenager to wear nothing but blue for several years in perpetual remembrance of Our Lady of Mercy. It didn't hurt, of course, that blue was also my favorite color.

After almost twenty years of dwelling in this world of devotional Catholicism, however, I moved on to the Newman Center at college. There the constellation of Mary and the saints, statues, medals, novenas and indulgences seemed to vanish overnight. In place of the rosary, Stations of the Cross and Forty Hours, I was confronted with new practices such as Bible study, the social justice committee, centering prayer and the Charismatic Renewal. It was a bewildering new landscape, which owed as much to the local parish's absorption of the Second Vatican Council as it did to my moving out of the second-generation European-American cultural "ghetto" of my youth. The Church I knew in my younger years had taken a giant step away from the sentimental, gentle piety of my experience, and had moved into something harshly cerebral—making new demands on my will and intellect. Religion was no longer a matter of *feeling*; rather, religion involved *thought* and *action*. I wasn't sure I liked the changes.

Within a matter of years, as I came to appreciate the Church's new self-understanding, I grew apart from Mary and her earlier stellar role in my spiritual life. I didn't know how to incorporate the quaintness of devotion to her into the appreciation I had gained for a biblically grounded, socially conscious, Spirit-led Church. I had no quarrel with Marian devotion; I just didn't know where it fit into the vision of Church I had acquired. Even after attending four years of seminary and boning up on systematic theology, liturgy, spirituality, Church history and Scripture, I couldn't find a way to incorporate the Marian experience I had been familiar with as a child into my adult life.

New Wine, New Wineskins

Like many Catholics caught in the breech between the Latin Mass and Vatican II, I floundered for a while, looking for the bridge that church leaders, consumed with the excitement of the Council, failed to provide between the "old" Church and the "new." Accustomed to the top-down executive style of leadership that had served the Church for generations, most pastors simply took orders and gave orders, expecting the usual obedience.

The changes of the Council were enacted with this same heavy-handedness, and many people got lost in the resulting confusion. Some repudiated the old style of Church entirely and embraced the new one as a restoration of truth. Others threw out both baby and bath water by rejecting both the changes and the Church altogether. Instead, they privately held on to "the faith of their fathers."

The ambivalence among priests in regard to the changes in the Church didn't help matters. I remember our pastor's words from the pulpit as he explained the turning around of the altar and the celebrating of Mass in English: "I don't like it any more than you do, but they tell us that's the way it's going to be."

As Pope Paul VI took pains to explain in his Marian document *Marialis Cultus* (1974), the Church never intended to ban devotional practices in the reform of the liturgy. Devotions were to be harmonized with the spirit of the reform, not suppressed. People who scorned the overly emotional elements of some traditional pious practices saw their elimination as a victory of sorts; however, these same folks felt no responsibility to fill the vacuum caused by the cessation of such spiritual disciplines.

It had always been the wisdom of the Church to blend longstanding teaching with new insight in a fruitful bond of broader understanding. The slammed-on-brakes approach of many parishes after the Council, however, did not reflect this practice. Long-overdue liturgical reform took on an urgency that sacrificed pastoral consideration in its enforcement. The result was what the late Cardinal Joseph Bernardin of Chicago lamented as the great unhealed fracture of the Church in our times: the lack of common ground between pre- and post-Vatican II Catholics. One side felt betrayed and abandoned; the other side was self-righteous, as those who lose their moorings to the past often are. The resulting suspicion and lack of charity on both sides was distinctly un-Christian.

My own slow creep back to middle ground was not unlike that of many others. I no longer find a home in an expression of piety focused almost exclusively on the otherworldly, nor am I attracted to the goal of fostering personal sanctity or racking up points for myself in heaven. But neither do I appreciate the pageantry of some contemporary expressions of liturgy that enthrall and entertain and instruct but do not exalt. I don't think I am alone in wanting to find a place in religion for my head, my heart and my hands. I find no comfort in saccharine spiritual images that are less holy than Hollywood. But the alternative cannot be a stripped-down ethics or spirituality that aims relentlessly at the concerns of this world, with no room for awe and mystery.

It is curious that Mary has reappeared on the scene—practically if not literally, as she has been known to do—to provide one path toward reconciliation of these polarized impulses. Like a patient mother, she is accustomed to being sidelined by her grown children for long periods of time, with no hard feelings. As a popular rosary T-shirt expresses it: "Call home! Your mother hasn't heard from you in decades."

Maybe Pope John Paul II's announcement of five new mysteries of the rosary is an invitation for some of us to "call home" and give Mary and the rosary a second look.

Why the Rosary?

Generations of Catholics now roam the Church with no experience of the rosary. Others put their beads down forty years ago and have taken them up only at funerals since then. My thirty-something sister, Evelyn, recalls praying the rosary one time, years ago, in an hour of adolescent desperation. All afternoon she had been in a state of emergency about getting to the new *Star Wars* movie, but no one had materialized with a ride to the theater. So she prayed the entire rosary with great feeling—and then the phone rang: A girlfriend had scored her mother's car! Although that experience gave Evie a sincere appreciation of the rosary, she decided to reserve such a powerful means of intercession for real emergencies.

Pope Paul VI reminded us that the rosary is a means and not an end in itself. We should not view the beads as a magic object or amulet, nor is the power of intercessory prayer a way of getting heaven on our side. Although the rosary is a prayer of intercession—an "asking" form of prayer—it is also properly understood as a form of meditation and contemplation. Pope Pius XII called the rosary "a compendium of the entire gospel," and Cardinal John Henry Newman noted it is a way of "holding in our hands all that we believe." As a means of transforming the gospel or the Creed into prayer, then, we can think of the rosary as a handy catechism for the road. Whether it is viewed as intercession, contemplation or instruction, the rosary is a pocket-sized expression of Christian faith.

To grasp this idea, consider the principal events of salvation accomplished in Christ: his Incarnation, Passion and Resurrection. As theologians explain it, Christ emptied himself of divinity to share in our humanity. This is the essence of the miracle of the Incarnation. Christ embraced suffering and death to remove the consequences of sin as an eternal barrier to union with God. This is the meaning of his Passion. Christ was exalted by God in the resurrection and will return in glory at the end of time to share this victory with those who believe in him. This is the hope of the Resurrection. In the Joyful, Sorrowful and Glorious Mysteries, we explore and celebrate these three movements of salvation.

The new Mysteries of Light, also called the Luminous Mysteries, provide the welcome addition of a spotlight on the public ministry of Jesus, which took place between the events recorded in the Joyful Mysteries, at the start of his mortal life, and those of the Sorrowful Mysteries, at its conclusion. The Incarnation finds its ultimate expression in these "illuminating" moments of epiphany that revealed the fullness of Jesus' identity all along the way.

As Pope Paul VI clearly emphasized, all Christian worship finds its origin in and takes its effectiveness from Christ and leads through Christ in the Spirit to the Father in Trinitarian fashion. This is as true of the rosary as it is of any other form of Christian prayer.

But the rosary's unique approach is its expression of the Christian story through the heart of Mary of Nazareth, who Scripture tells us was the first to treasure and ponder these events. With Mary, we contemplate the rhythms of human life—its cycles of happiness and grief, expectation and loss, sin and inexplicable grace—along with their transfigured counterparts in the life of Jesus. As the premier disciple and model of the Church, Mary shows us how to place all the pieces of our personal stories, even those that are sharp-edged, into the greater story of salvation.

Even the historical abuses of Marian prayer are instructive in the parameters they establish for devotional practice as a whole. Marian *minimalism*, the devaluation of her human response to God's initiative, is as much to be avoided as *maximalism*, which overemphasizes Mary to the diminishment of Christ. Because of the supreme significance God places on human free will, humanity is a free and full participant in the work of grace. The example of Mary demonstrates how much can be accomplished when one of us responds without reservation to God's invitation. Such cooperation cannot be underestimated.

The History of the Rosary
Most of us credit Saint Dominic with the rosary's beginnings, and certainly the Dominicans of the sixteenth century did the lion's share of fostering the traditional form of the rosary as we know it. But the evolution of this prayer form had its roots in earlier practices.

The Latin word *rosarium*, meaning rose garden, was used for collections of devotional texts, popular by the fourteenth century. Three hundred years earlier, however, praying the *paternosters* already was commonly known as "the poor man's breviary." The traditional monastic practice of reciting the entire 150 psalms on a daily or weekly cycle was beyond the general population, illiterate and hardworking as they were. Instead the devout prayed 150 Our Fathers as they labored, counting them off on strings of beads or knots.

Such devotions were more accessible than the cerebral Latin liturgy, which offered little room for lay participation. Seeking a bridge between intellectual teaching and a vital experience of faith, people flocked to novenas rather than Mass; to the exposition of the Blessed Sacrament rather than receiving the Eucharist; and to the ritual application of holy water while putting off baptism until their deathbeds. Such devotions met the felt need that the more formal sacramental practices failed to address.

In the eleventh century, five "Joys of Mary" were popularly celebrated, paired neatly with the liturgical feasts of the Annunciation, the Nativity, the Triduum, the Ascension and the Assumption. A century later, two more Joys were added—the adoration of the Magi and the sending of the Holy Spirit—to complete a seven-day "office." It was at this time that the Hail Mary was incorporated into this devotional series.

The evolution of the devotion continued in the thirteenth century, with the Franciscans and the Servites promoting the "Seven Delights of Mary," which included the addition of the Visitation. The Cistercians offered an expanded series of fifteen "Joys of Mary," centered in Christ and celebrated with Scripture, liturgy and contemplation in accordance with Saint Bernard's instruction. It took a Dominican of the fourteenth century, Blessed Henry Suso, to promote devotion to the "Sorrows of Mary," which included the massacre of the Innocents and the prophecy of Simeon.

Up to then the historical events of Mary's recollection had dominated the world of devotion, but in the fifteenth century the "Seven Celestial Joys of Mary" became popular, commemorating her role in the communion of saints and her key intercession in prayer. The combination of terrestrial and celestial events contained the seed of the rosary's present form, in which two non-biblical celestial moments round out the Glorious Mysteries.

We owe the rosary in its traditional form to Dominican Alain Roche of the fifteenth century. He spread the "New Psalter of the Virgin," with its fifteen mysteries concerning the fundamental aspects of faith in Jesus Christ and the ramifications of this faith on the life of the Church. From that time on, the practice of praying the rosary mirrored a virtual liturgical year as well as a short course in Christian faith.

The Rosary as Prayer

The early church used these familiar words from Luke's Gospel in its liturgies:

> *Hail Mary, full of grace, the Lord is with thee. Blessed art thou amongst women, and blessed is the fruit of thy womb (Luke 1:28, 42).*

This combination of the angel's greeting with Elizabeth's greeting to Mary was a common prayer in the Church of the West until the thirteenth century, when this prayer of supplication was added:

> *Holy Mary, Mother of God, pray for us sinners, now and at the hour of our death.*

In full, these words came to constitute what the Church calls the "Hail Mary."

Pope Paul VI, appealing to the image of a loom, called the Hail Mary the "warp" on which the rosary's mysteries are woven. In this brief prayer we acknowledge the two sides to the Incarnation: how the Son of the Virgin is likewise the Son of God. Prayed 150 times in the traditional rosary, the Hail Mary shares a kinship with the Psalter and the origins of monastic prayer. As Pope Paul VI noted, the prayer hinges on Jesus as its center of gravity. Our intercession through Mary is dynamically grounded in Jesus, just as her own identity within salvation history is rooted in him.

As a gospel prayer of praise, as a form of petition, and as a means to contemplation, the rosary benefits from a quiet rhythm and lingering pace. Each part contributes respectfully to the whole. The mysteries function as icons to the gospel message, just as Jesus serves as the human face of God. Silence and vocal prayer are its alternating energies. Scripture is followed by prayer for the grace to know the fruits of each mystery, that we may "imitate what they contain and obtain what they promise," as the well-known prayer from the Litany of Loreto phrases it. The undulating repetitions remind us that Jesus taught the value of persistent prayer, in the parable of the widow as well as in his encounter with the Canaanite woman. The gentle rhythm also establishes the atmosphere of meditation, which the *Catechism of the Catholic Church* calls above all a quest (see no. 2705). Through this quest we seek the engagement of thought, imagination, emotion and desire in order to move from the state of simple reflection to union with Christ. Since Mary was the first person to experience that union, who can more perfectly show us the way?

Communal recitation of the rosary leads naturally to the liturgy and is a useful preparation for it. The practice of the rosary is neither identical to the Eucharist nor opposed to it, as it gathers its motivating force from liturgy but does not duplicate its saving action. Pope Paul VI counsels against praying the rosary during Mass or in place of it, yet he insists that the practice of saying the rosary regularly does assist us in the growth in grace, which is at the heart of our friendship with God.

Mary and the Church
Two things must be stated clearly before all else: What we say about Mary is always rooted in what we believe about Jesus and cannot be separated from him; and what we say about Mary also is true of the Church and therefore sheds light on our vocation in the world. The documents of the Second Vatican Council present Mary as the realization of the Church (see *Lumen Gentium,* nos. 53, 63). John's Gospel was first to note that the beloved disciple was given to the mother as surely as the mother was entrusted to the care of the disciple by Jesus himself at the cross. As Saint Augustine observed, Mary, as Mother of the Church, continues to bring about the birth of all believers. In her singular trust, love, service and attention to God's will, Mary embodies and models the Christian vocation.

Although Mary's example was greatly admired and venerated in previous generations, it has been impossible not to observe the reservations attending Marian emphasis in recent times. Pope Paul VI addressed the problem perceptively in this pastoral analysis:

Devotion to the Blessed Virgin must also pay close attention to certain findings of the human sciences.... The picture of the Blessed Virgin presented in a certain type of devotional literature cannot be easily reconciled with today's lifestyle, especially the way women live today. In the home, woman's equality and co-responsibility with man in the running of the family are being justly recognized by laws and the evolution of customs. In the sphere of politics, women have in many countries gained a position in public life equal to that of men. In the social field women are at work in a whole range of different employments, getting further away every day from the restricted surroundings of the home. In the cultural field new possibilities are opening up for women in scientific research and intellectual activities.

In consequence of these phenomena some people are becoming disenchanted with devotion to the Blessed Virgin and finding it difficult to take as an example Mary of Nazareth, because the horizons of her life, so they say, seem rather restricted in comparison with the vast spheres of activity open to humankind today (*Marialis Cultus,* no. 34).

As Pope Paul VI submits, the point of offering Mary as an example was never to suggest that we imitate the life she led, with its unique themes and circumstances. Rather, the driving force of her actions—charity and the spirit of service—impelled her to become the first and most perfect disciple, the one who heard the word of God and acted upon it like no other person in history. Those are the qualities we are to emulate—but in a way that reflects our own times. As the pope goes on to suggest, it is normal for each generation to express its sentiments about the mother of Jesus in a manner appropriate and useful to its age.

Marialis Cultus recommends a few ways modern women might

find a suitable ally and welcome role model in Mary of Nazareth. First, the example of Mary is one of a woman taken into dialogue with God. Her active and responsible consent is sought before the divine operation can be put into effect. This is no insignificant sideshow of human history. Rather, that "event of world importance" is in fact the Incarnation (see no. 37). Contemporary women are likewise anxious to participate fully in the affairs of the world community with real authority to make decisions and to have the power to effect substantial change.

Second, in her *Magnificat* Mary presents herself as far from the timid, submissive woman of some pious stereotypes. She advocates for the humble and oppressed, proclaiming the God who vindicates the poor by removing the powerful from positions of privilege for the sake of the poor. This prophetic woman also demonstrates great character and strength in persevering through poverty and suffering, flight and exile, and is no stranger to the realities of an unjust society. This same woman helps strengthen the faith of the apostolic community by her actions at Cana (see the meditation on the second Luminous Mystery), by her ongoing presence and prayer at the cross and at Pentecost, and ultimately in her extended and universal role as Mother of the Church.

How to Pray These Mysteries

The addition of five new mysteries to the rosary presents the question of a reorganization of the traditional order of the prayer. Although the mysteries of the rosary can be prayed all at once in "chronological" order—Joyful, Luminous, Sorrowful and Glorious—many will want to continue the practice of praying one set of the mysteries a day. Pope John Paul II has recommended this order for those who seek a purposeful daily assignment for the mysteries:

- The Joyful Mysteries are prayed on Mondays and Saturdays.
- The Sorrowful Mysteries are prayed Tuesdays and Fridays.

- The Glorious Mysteries are prayed on Wednesdays and Sundays.
- The Luminous Mysteries are prayed on Thursdays.

This reassignment, while not chronological, has the liturgical advantage of returning Mary's traditional day, Saturday, to meditation on her particular mysteries; honoring Fridays with the memorial of the cross; and reuniting each Sunday with the remembrance of Easter in the Glorious Mysteries. The pope recognizes that pastoral or personal applications may warrant a different ordering, which is left to the freedom of the individual.

The Spirit of Our Meditations

What is most important in praying the twenty mysteries of the rosary is not the order but the spirit of each set of meditations.

The joy expressed abundantly in the Gospel of Luke is celebrated fervently in the *Joyful Mysteries;* but as with the original "Joys of Mary," that does not imply only happy recollections. As Pope John Paul II suggests, Christian joy is not always uncomplicated and cannot be confused with a life free from care. Contained in each drama of the Joyful Mysteries is its contradiction. The angel's Annunciation brings challenging and not altogether welcome news to the young and unmarried Mary. Mary's *Magnificat*, delivered during the Visitation, acknowledges the injustice and suffering that exists in our divided world. The birth of Jesus leads to the slaughter of innocents. When Jesus is presented in the Temple, his parents are not only blessed but warned of the difficult road ahead. The finding of the boy Jesus comes only after the losing of him. In the midst of these contradictions, Christian faith is bound to joy with the confidence that to God alone belongs the victory.

The *Luminous Mysteries* center on the revelation that Christ is our Eternal Light and that in his face we somehow behold the actual face of God. In 1957, Blessed Father George Preca of Malta was inspired to offer a set of meditations on the public ministry of Jesus to include in the rosary. His list includes the entire Beatitudes, while Pope John Paul II has chosen a more focused contemplation on Jesus' proclamation of the kingdom and call to repentance. The pope has brought the fruit of Father Preca's reflections to a wider audience through the promotion of these mysteries and by beatifying the priest. We are now invited to view these little epiphanies of understanding from the public life of Jesus that can help lead all seekers to the fullness of faith. The five episodes serve as five doors to admit fresh recognition of "the person of Jesus" as our revealed "Christ of faith," in theologian Karl Rahner's distinct phrases.

In the *Sorrowful Mysteries,* perhaps dearest to every human heart because of the singular way grief brings us to prayer, the Church contemplates the death of the faithful, both personally and profoundly, through the mystery of the cross. Once again we "behold the man," and in beholding the suffering Lord we see how God holds human misery close in an intimate encounter of compassion and shared anguish. In the hymn *Stabat Mater,* Mary stubbornly retains her place at the foot of the cross. Through the life of the Church, as we take up the sorrows of the world, we are grateful that our Mother remains close at hand, "her station keeping," as the hymn proclaims.

Through contemplation of the *Glorious Mysteries,* we are renewed in the central mystery of our faith: The Crucified One is also the Risen One! Just as Jesus is raised to glory, we see the Church ascend to new life in Pentecost and are guaranteed our supreme realization in the prefiguration of Mary's assumption into heaven and her crowning as Queen of Heaven.

Altogether, these mysteries lead us to contemplate, in Pope John Paul II's words, "the ocean of joy and light, suffering and glory" that encompasses our experience and is contained in the depths of the heart of Christ. What remains is for us to reflect on these mysteries for ourselves.

The Joyful Mysteries

The First Joyful Mystery

The Annunciation

God sent the angel Gabriel to a town in Galilee called Nazareth, to the home of a young woman, Mary, promised in marriage to a man named Joseph of the house of David. The angel came to Mary and said, "Hail, favored one! The Lord is with you." But she was deeply troubled at these words and wondered what this greeting might mean. Then the angel said to her, "Do not be afraid, Mary, for you have found favor with God. Behold, you will conceive and bear a son, and you shall name him Jesus. He will be called Son of the Most High. God will give him the throne of David his father, and of his kingdom there will be no end."

Mary asked, "How can this be, since I am a virgin?" The angel replied, "The holy Spirit will come upon you, and the power of the Most High will overshadow you. The child to be born will be called holy, the Son of God. And see, Elizabeth, your kinswoman, has conceived a son in her old age, and she who was called barren is in her sixth month, for nothing is impossible for God."

Mary said, "Behold, I am the handmaid of the Lord. Let it be done to me as you say." Then the angel left her.

—*the Gospel of Luke*

Saint Bernard of Clairvaux preached that there were only four virtues: humility, humility, humility and humility. Most of us find it hard to stomach even one of these. Possibly we confuse humility with low self-esteem or, worse, with being humiliated. But humility is not about thinking ill of ourselves or being brought low by others. Humility is about bending low to lift others up.

We learn true humility in the great hymn that Saint Paul quotes in Philippians (see 2:6–11). Jesus who did not cling to his divinity emptied himself to embrace our humanity. He accepted the cross, not because it is good to be oppressed but to free us from the state of oppression caused by sin. Just as Jesus is lifted up in the Resurrection, so we too are raised to the hope of new life. The humble servant swings low but aims high.

The Annunciation is a celebration of such humility demonstrated by an adolescent girl twenty centuries ago. What would a modern teenager do, unexpectedly confronted with the powers of heaven? What would any of us do if God's will became known to us spectacularly and concretely in a moment's time? We like to think we would answer as Mary does in pronouncing her famous *fiat*, her simple and humble "let it be." But humility does not start with words. As Jesus revealed, we cannot take on the will of God without first emptying ourselves of our own plans. This aspect of humility is perhaps harder than any other. After all, how many of us want to give up our own agenda, even for a few hours? Fewer of us, we can imagine, would surrender our dreams and plans for a lifetime.

***

As every parent learns, having a child alters the course of one's entire life path. Welcoming a child means initial physical encumbrance, which is followed by a long season of sleepless nights and homebound days. Then there are years of accountability, worry, constant presence, financial responsibility, ongoing modeling of behavior and values, and the delicate burden of being the center of the whole emotional world for another. It is a wonder people are brave enough to become parents at all. Of course, some parents are unable or unwilling to see it through, leading to the sorrowful realities of abortion, abandoned children, single-parent households, or emotionally unavailable, neglectful or abusive mothers and fathers. Clearly, the school of committed parenting is the fast lane to the virtue of humility. Self-emptying for the long haul is the name of the game.

Those who are not parents or whose active parenting days are over can exercise this virtue by creating a space in their lives to welcome the other: "the stranger, the widow, and the orphan" in biblical terms. A vast number of wanderers roam our society in need of roots, community, belonging and hospitality. A smile flashed at a harried woman in the grocery store, a gift purchased for an unknown child whose name hangs on the Christmas Giving Tree, a dinner invitation offered to a loner who rarely receives such invitations, and the thousand inconveniences we accept on behalf of those we know and love (or don't love)—all of these are ways we answer the call to humility. By these acts, we allow our agenda to be displaced for the sake of another, who is ultimately Christ in our midst.

***

Saint Ignatius of Antioch wrote that the virgin birth and even the death of Jesus are mysteries that escaped the notice of "the prince of this world," because they were accomplished in God's silence. Even Scripture is silent on precisely how the virgin birth was achieved, and centuries of debate have shed no new light on the matter. What Scripture does tell us is that the girl who said "yes" exchanged emptiness for fullness. She understood that choosing God's way over hers made her more of who she was, not less. For who knows the truth of who we are better than the One who called us into being? The fullness of Mary's womb for a time brought forth the absolute "fullness of time" that all creation had been groaning for since the advent of sin. Mary's vocation as Mother of Mercy, discovered much later, knew its origins here. We can see that Mary did not deny herself in embracing God's will. Rather, she found herself.

***

In God's silence, beyond human reason, in the realm of what

we call mystery, Mary agreed to accept an incomprehensible "over-shadowing" and a destiny she could scarcely understand. Yet in laying down her will and embracing God's purpose she not only discovered her own vocation but became a guide along the way of humility. Consider how closely these phrases echo one another: "Let it be done to me according to your will;" "Your kingdom come, your will be done;" "Not my will, but yours, be done." As Mary became enveloped in the way of God, it became possible for her to teach that way to her Son. Jesus, in turn, instructed his disciples in the Lord's Prayer to pray for the grace to do God's will. And he found his own vocation as the savior of sinners when he surrendered his will completely—as his mother had taught him—in the garden of Gethsemane. The spirit of humility, although its origins are modest, widens to admit the God of every possibility through its little door.

The Second Joyful Mystery

The Visitation

Mary set out in haste to a Judean town in the hill country, where she entered the house of Zechariah and greeted Elizabeth. When Elizabeth heard Mary's greeting, the child leaped in her womb. Elizabeth, filled with the Holy Spirit, exclaimed, "Blessed are you among women, and blessed is the fruit of your womb! And how can this be, that the mother of my Lord should come to me? For no sooner had your greeting sounded in my ears, than the baby in my womb leaped for joy. And blessed is she who believed that the Lord's word to her would be fulfilled."

And Mary replied, "My soul proclaims the greatness of God, and my spirit rejoices in God my savior."

—the Gospel of Luke

From time to time, even from the unlikeliest corners of our community, we hear people do it: express gratitude for the spouse who is always there for them; ponder how fortunate they are to come from a loving family; express relief at having found work that is meaningful to them; revel in the change of seasons; rejoice at the freedom of the upcoming weekend. By any other name, people who are aware of goodness in their lives are counting their blessings.

What do you count among the blessings visited upon you? Name the people who have been angels of grace for you in times of sorrow or celebration. Consider the beauty that has come your way and the wonders you have seen. Number the times you were rescued from the consequences of your own poor choices. Admit the occasions when good things happened that you might not have thought you had earned or even deserved. Most of us, if we spend enough time in contemplation, will count a whole rosary of blessings that have been given to us free of charge—which is the only way real blessings arrive.

***

But what might it mean not simply to *receive* a blessing but to *be* one? Mary of Nazareth was not the first person in the Bible to know that honor. The original man of blessing was Abraham, one of the most significant figures in Hebrew Scripture. God once made a wager with Abraham that must have seemed as remarkable to the old man as the message Gabriel would later bring to the young woman Mary. "Leave your father's house and your homeland," God told Abraham, "and go to a land I will show you." And in return, God promised him:

> *I will make of you a great nation, and I will bless you and make your name great, so that you will be a blessing. I will bless those who bless you, and the one who curses you I will curse; and in you all the families of the earth shall be blessed (Genesis 12:2–3).*

As rare and strange as all that might sound to anyone, it was twice as confounding to Abraham. First, he didn't know this God who spoke to him. Abraham came from the land of Ur, where the gods were plentiful. Second, he was married to a woman he'd loved for more than half a century, yet he and Sarah had no children. What this God was suggesting seemed ridiculous in every respect. Why should an obscure man like Abraham ever be a blessing to all the earth? Yet the thing about Abraham, despite the absurdities, is that *he went*. By God and in faith, he packed his stuff and undertook the journey.

***

And all these many centuries later a young girl in the land to which Abraham had been led was once more called a blessing. What would God intend by this? Mary knew it meant something wonderful to be blessed among women, and in her *Magnificat* she claimed the blessing for all generations, echoing the promise made to Abraham. She compared herself to her people Israel, forever heirs to Abraham's special covenant with God. Like Abraham, she understood that the great things being done for her would extend far beyond her in time and space. They would have repercussions for the poor and the lowly, the powerless and the hungry. Young Mary, in comparing herself to the great and holy father of her nation, embraced a vision many would have seen as unsuitably ambitious for anyone, much less a person of her age, gender and position in society. Mary did not exalt herself, however; she knew it was God who worked these incredible wonders through her. So she too was willing to risk an astonishing journey—with God and in faith.

***

Jesus would later publicly acknowledge the richness of such faith as he taught the crowds. A woman caught up in the wonder of his teaching cried out to Jesus, "Blessed is the womb that carried you, and the breasts that nursed you!" She meant no disrespect. It was then, as now, a kindness to speak well of someone's mother, just as it is the worst form of insult to speak badly of her. But Jesus wanted it to be clear that the real achievement of his mother extended well past her biological role in bearing him. "Blessed are those who hear the word of God and keep it," he corrected his admirer (Luke 11:27–28).

***

What makes the Visitation so delightful for contemplation is the way two women—one so young and full of the excitement of the future, one old and wise with the experience of the past—find in each other an instant alliance and rapport based on their mutual appreciation of divine mystery. Elizabeth feels the movement in her womb and declares the blessing she is witnessing. Mary acknowledges the blessing and proclaims the handiwork of God.

There is no hesitation between them, no need for explanations about what is going on. Insecurity and rationalization are for those who lack trust in the journey on which God is leading them. These women plunge forward into the mystery, body and soul, as unreservedly as they fall into each other's arms. When God is at work, talk is beside the point. It is more appropriate, as Mary knew, to sing!

The Third Joyful Mystery

The Nativity of Jesus

A decree went out from Caesar Augustus that the whole world should be enrolled in a census. So all went, each to his own town. And Joseph also went up from Nazareth in Galilee to the city of David called Bethlehem in Judea, because he was of the house of David. There he would be enrolled with Mary, his betrothed, who was with child. While they were there, the time came for her to have her child, and she gave birth to her firstborn son. She wrapped him in swaddling clothes and laid him in a manger, for there was no room for them in the place where travelers lodged.

There were shepherds in that region living in the fields, keeping watch over their flocks by night. The angel of the Lord appeared to them, and the glory of the Lord shone around them, and they were terrified. But the angel said, "Do not be afraid; for behold, I am bringing you good news of great joy that will be for all people. For today in the city of David a savior has been born for you who is Messiah and Lord."

—*the Gospel of Luke*

A Child is born for us. A Son is given to us. What we hear at the heart of this mystery of Incarnation is that God moved to bring forth this marvel for *us*. Certainly, God did not need to have a personal experience of being flesh and blood. The Creator of the Universe could have saved the world by any number of means. What is wonderful in this event, what catches our breath, is the same message given to the shepherds minding their own business in the fields that night: Good news has arrived that is for *all people*; a Savior has arrived not for his own sake but for *our sakes*.

The shepherds were speechless. *No one* ever did anything on *their* behalf! They were loners and outsiders, unused to being included in human plans, much less those of the Lord of the Universe. Why should a Savior come for them? Why should heaven and earth be moved for their sake? The shepherds in Luke's story saw the incongruity we sometimes miss: how the angels reported this world-changing event straightaway to the most forgotten and marginalized folk. In Matthew's version, by contrast, the revelation is noted first by kings. But we can find the harmony in these two distinct stories by listening to the angel's words. Whether the poor have the good news preached to them or the heavens announce it to the perceptive eye of educated men of the East, the message of the angel stands firm. This great joy is *for all people.* Anyone who hears and understands this news is the intended recipient.

***

How did such wonder come about? It all started with the census, a numbers game forbidden to Jews by law. The Hebrew Scripture made it clear that the number of the people of Israel was not to be counted, for such knowledge would lead to pride in the nation's strength and a sense of possessiveness on the part of rulers. In truth the nation belonged to God alone, who was to be Israel's only strength. Rome, of course, was oblivious to this. Caesar sought an estimate of how many potential rebels he had out there in the far reaches of his empire or perhaps how many pockets he could pick with his taxes. He did not care for Israel's law, much less Israel's God.

But God has always been pleased to use the movements of politics and history to the divine advantage. Rome might pursue its census, but God would put a celestial thumb on the scale and offset the sum. A Child was born in a stable, an apparently negligible addition to the final tally on the sheet that year. That humble little family altogether did not amount to more than three strokes in an anonymous column. If only Caesar had understood that God delights in taking the small, weak and finite and multiplying it beyond counting. Mathematicians and accountants, stand back!

***

The traditional virtue assigned to praying this mystery of the rosary is the spirit of poverty. No one wants to be poor, and no one prays to become so. But consider what God does with human poverty. God takes an infertile couple like Abraham and Sarah and makes of them a holy nation. God transforms Moses, a Hebrew-born slave, into a prince of Egypt. God chooses the shepherd boy David to be a great king over Israel. God saves a whole people through the actions of a devout widow, Judith. God pairs a courageous adolescent girl and a faithful carpenter from Nazareth and brings forth the Prince of Peace in a stable in the inhospitable town of Bethlehem. When we recognize what God can do with poverty, we might find the courage to pray to be heartily poor for the sake of heaven's purposes.

***

In the end, the story of the Nativity can be seen as another miracle of multiplication—God's oldest and favorite way of demonstrating generosity. What is small becomes immense. What seems irrelevant is most important. The tiny Child contains infinity, and the Helpless One is the source of salvation for all. A drama that takes place in an inconspicuous corner of the empire will assume center stage in the history of those who believe. A carpenter's son will be honored—and hunted—by kings, and finally, remarkably, named a King himself as he hangs dying in infamy. The stone that the builders reject will become the cornerstone. This is what God does with our poverty.

Mary collaborates in God's wonderful reversal, embracing the poverty of not knowing what is to become of her and her Child after she cedes her will to the gracious mystery. Because she is faithful in small matters, she is put in charge of larger ones. Because she bravely accepts heaven's bargain and gives birth to Jesus, she remains today the Mother of the Mystical Body of Christ, the Church. Her maternity is writ large across the centuries. And what was done for Mary, we are always told, is done for us who are the Church as well.

Are we prepared to hear this? And are we ready to receive it as good news? For today is born a Savior *for us*—not for other folk in other times but right here and right now. This Savior is for all people, and this Savior chooses to start his ministry in the territory of the poor.

Where is the region of our personal poverty, and is it large enough for him to pitch his tent there and begin?

The Fourth Joyful Mystery

The Presentation in the Temple

When the time came for their purification according to the law of Moses, Mary and Joseph brought Jesus up to Jerusalem to present him to the Lord. Now there was a man in Jerusalem named Simeon who was righteous and devout. He looked forward to the consolation of Israel, and the Holy Spirit rested on him. It had been revealed to him by the Holy Spirit that he would not see death before he had seen the Lord's Messiah. Guided by the Spirit, Simeon came to the temple, took the child Jesus in his arms, and praised God, saying:

"Master, now you let your servant go in peace, according to your word; for my eyes have seen your salvation, which you have prepared in the sight of every people, a light to reveal you to the Gentiles, and for the glory of your people Israel."

The child's father and mother were amazed at what was being said about him. Then Simeon blessed them and said to his mother Mary, "This child is destined for the rise and fall of many in Israel, and to be a sign of contradiction so that the hearts of many will be revealed. And a sword will pierce your own soul too."

—the Gospel of Luke

Life contains few neat and proper categories. In our experience of life there are joys and sorrows, failures and triumphs, but they don't stay in separate corners of the room or remain out of conscious memory when we are engaged in a present encounter. Each happiness is tempered by the possibility of loss. Every grief is made bearable with the hope of tomorrow or the comfort of the past. Our personal mysteries, we might say, are not pure instances of one emotion or another. Human experience is more often a medley of many emotional colors flowing together.

So we are not surprised to hear in this Joyful Mystery the distant trumpet of sorrow to come. The earliest collections of devotions surrounding Mary were known as her "joys" or "delights," yet they always included the Passion of Jesus. In fact, we can scarcely speak of Mary's Son without mention of his crucifixion. This was illustrated simply in a house I saw decorated for Christmas a number of years ago. A string of lights had been used to form the jagged sketch of a pine tree and a second string had been hung "inside" the tree in the shape of a cross. And there the two images remained, one contained within the other—Christmas and the crucifixion proclaimed at once. Surely the Incarnation of Jesus contained his death just as plainly; every mortal life begins with the absolute guarantee of death to follow. This was the bargain God accepted when the Word chose to become flesh and dwell among us.

***

We are not shaken, then, when Mary and Joseph take their Child to the Temple for the purification rites and encounter a holy man and his discomforting message. Like most parents, Mary and Joseph would prefer a blessing for their child and perhaps a few encouraging words about what is to come. Instead Simeon blesses *them* and foresees that the road ahead will be difficult. This prophet could have called Jesus by so many names: Prince of Peace, Hope of Sinners, Son of the Most High. He chooses, however, to call Jesus a "sign of contradiction"—not what parents hope to hear said of their child. Simeon's image of a sword passing through Mary's heart and soul probably doesn't assuage their concern.

When we hold a baby in our arms we are tempted to stay in the moment, enjoying the pleasure of this tiny life, basking in an innocence of which none of us has any personal memory. It is hard to consider the childhood illnesses, troubled adolescence, difficult career choices and adult crises this little creature may face. A parent does not wish to imagine that the child in his or her arms may one day suffer injury, loss or failure. How much more incomprehensible is the idea that this new life will someday end in death? The crucifixion of Jesus may be implicit in the Incarnation, but Mary and Joseph surely do not go to the Temple with death in mind.

***

The drama mixed with the joy of the Presentation foreshadows the Sorrowful Mysteries to come. Artists have often sensed this inseparable mixture. The Madonna who holds her lovely Son in her arms is rarely portrayed as smiling. In fact, she is often depicted as very sad, as in the Russian Virgin of Vladimir. In this icon, we see the Mother almost inconsolable, as the small Child in her arms reaches his tiny hand around her neck to comfort her.

One of the insights of Michelangelo's genius was to transfer the woe of the young Mother to his *Pieta*. Here again Mary holds her Son in her arms—but this is quite a different scene. Mary has not aged a day since she held her Infant. We see the familiar quiet dignity and reserved expression of pain as she gathers to herself the proportionately smaller body of her adult Son. We perceive that she has always held her Son this way, pierced by that early sword of knowing what was to come in the service of God's will. She accepts this suffering, then and now, as threads in a seamless garment of mysteries to be revealed in glory not yet visible to the eye.

Saint Bernard once prayed on the Feast of the Presentation, "Offer your Son, holy Virgin, and present to the Lord the blessed fruit of your womb." Hidden in this early offering at the Temple is the image of the *Pieta*, like the cross inside the Christmas tree. These same arms bear the Boy she would always receive, just like this, wrapped in divine mysteries too deep to express and more than any human embrace can hold.

In the same way, we the faithful bring our joys and losses together before God, recognizing the Paschal Mystery in every aspect of our humanity. We believe that God is present not only in our strength but also in our weakness—most of all in our weakness. We see the God of triumph in our losses and the God of compassion in our suffering. We know there is no time when God is absent, only moments when we find the divine presence beyond the grasp of our reason. Like Mary in the Temple, we present our utmost vulnerability to God in the holy place. Our pierced soul belongs there in its naked struggle, even if we think it is not proper or perhaps downright shameful for God to see us this way. God sends a light of revelation and the hope of glory to all who turn toward Jesus. We have nothing to fear in presenting ourselves honestly and openly in every season the heart can know.

The Fifth Joyful Mystery

The Finding of Jesus in the Temple

When Jesus was twelve years old, his parents took him up to Jerusalem for the festival of the Passover. After the festival ended, they started for home, but the boy Jesus stayed behind in Jerusalem, though his parents did not know it. Assuming he was in the group of travelers, they went a day's journey. Then they looked for him among their relatives and friends, and when they did not find him they returned to the city to search for him. After three days they found him in the temple, sitting among the teachers, listening to them and asking questions. And all who heard him were amazed at his understanding.

His mother said to him: "Son, why have you treated us like this? Your father and I have been searching for you in great anxiety." He said to them, "Why were you searching for me? Did you not know that I must be in my Father's house?" But they did not understand what he said to them. Then Jesus went down with them to Nazareth and was obedient to them. His mother meanwhile treasured all these things in her heart.

—the Gospel of Luke

Who among us has not lost Jesus from time to time amid the ebb and flow of our lives? Who has not moved away from where he sits, at the center of teaching and tradition, and gone another way, straying from the essence of our faith?

Many Catholics report a season of lapse, sometimes for months but often for years, when faith assumed a marginal if not irrelevant position among their concerns and priorities. The lapse may begin in adolescence, when authority is routinely called into question. It may take place during the early years of career building, when the pursuit of success makes teachings about humility and self-emptying seem archaic and counterproductive. Young parents find church attendance hard to fit into the rhythms of childcare; and once it is interrupted the habit of churchgoing may be challenging to resume. Sometimes a move to a new city or parish may alter a relationship to the community of faith that was once a source of nourishment and support. Some of us are tempted to leave the path of discipleship because life seems so good without it. Others are equally tempted to abandon faith when life seems so bad despite it. And as we shuffle and reshuffle the priorities of our days, Jesus might well be overlooked.

***

The way it happened for Joseph and Mary sounds ludicrous to modern ears. Who could misplace a twelve-year-old for a whole day? How could his parents rest assured that he was safe somewhere among the relatives and fellow travelers? Our contemporary obsession with the welfare of our children and our fear of strangers make it hard to remember a time when children were raised by the whole village and the extended household was the rule, not the exception. Jesus lived in a time and culture when a boy was not constantly plastered to the side of his mother or father for fear of abduction or harm. At any rate, even twelve-year-old boys of our acquaintance do not tolerate this kind of coddling. In an age when men and women traveled in separate clusters and older boys were free to be in either camp, it would be simple enough for a child to go missing for at least that long.

There comes a moment in every child's life when he or she asserts independence, an hour when every parent realizes the authority he or she wields is losing its power to compel or persuade. This was such an hour for the holy family. How does a "holy" family respond to this exercise of autonomy and reassessment of roles and relationships? With mutual respect. After asserting his right and responsibility to choose as he did, Jesus submits to his parents and returns home with them.

But things are different now. Jesus has revealed that his sense of family goes beyond kinship, hinting that his "mother and brothers and sisters" will be those who, like him, honor God's authority above all others. Mary, for her part, remembers this day as particularly significant. She treasures it, for she had once made a choice not unlike the one her Son was making.

***

For a moment, we could say, it was not Jesus who was lost but his parents. They had forgotten—as parents can be forgiven for doing—that their Child did not belong to them. They had to recall that their Son did not exist to serve their expectations but that he, like them, was at the common service of the God who brought them all together for a greater purpose. It is easy to lose sight of the simple truth that other people do not exist for any purpose of ours. Children make this mistake about their parents as often as parents make it regarding their children. Spouses project this understanding onto each other, and friends do it to friends. "Why isn't she taking care of me? Why doesn't he see that I need him to listen? Why aren't they here for me when I am in trouble? Why won't they change and become what I want them to be?"

Just as we are in danger of losing Jesus by reducing his significance in our lives, we can lose one another in our attempts to possess, objectify or use one another. The smaller we make something, the harder it is to find. When we shrink the Lord to manageable size or cram others into compartments of our own making, we run the risk of finding ourselves very alone indeed.

***

In the traditional practice of the rosary, the virtue of piety is to be gained from contemplating this mystery. Genuine piety isn't about making sweet faces in church or bankrolling a mountain of prayers. The mutual respect Jesus and his parents offered to one another and to God in the Temple is more like it. Piety is knowing how to behave in the presence of the sacred. Jesus knew it and so honored both God and his parents in his actions. Joseph and Mary, steeped in the practice of piety through years of such choices, understood it was time to step aside and allow their Son to pursue the path God was leading him on. This kind of piety keeps God at the center of the dynamic of relationships and permits both God and others to be free agents instead of captives of our expectations and demands. The more authentically pious we become, the harder it will be for us to ever lose Jesus for long.

The Luminous Mysteries

The First Luminous Mystery

The Baptism of Jesus

John the Baptizer appeared in the wilderness, as prophecy had foretold:

> See, I am sending my messenger ahead of you.
> He is the voice crying in the desert:
> "Prepare the way of the Lord! Make straight
> his paths!"

The whole Judean countryside and all from Jerusalem were going out to him to confess their sins and be baptized in the river. John was clothed with camel's hair and wore a leather belt at his waist. He fed on locusts and wild honey. John declared: "The one who is to come is more powerful than I; I am not worthy to untie his sandals. I baptize with water. He will baptize you with the Holy Spirit and with fire!"

Jesus came from Nazareth to be baptized by John. As he rose from the water he saw the heavens torn open, and the Spirit descending on him like a dove. A voice from heaven proclaimed: "You are my Son, the Beloved. With you I am well pleased."

—the Gospels of Matthew, Mark and Luke

Being finite creatures locked into a moment of history, we admit to a certain prejudice regarding time. We like to know what time it is, so we hoist clocks onto our church towers, fasten them to every wall and strap them to our wrists. Most of all, we want to know at what point in time something has happened or is likely to happen: When does the party begin? Will the baby be born soon? How much longer can we expect to live?

The business of time is no light matter for people strapped to the motion of the clock and its relentless destiny in the future. So when it comes to religion, the "when" of things is crucial to our understanding. Christians ask questions such as: When did Jesus know he was God? At what moment are we definitively saved? Is the end of the world going to come shortly?

Time is a serious matter for mortals. Every second of the day, every choice we make is dependent upon the limitations of this fundamental dimension of our reality. When it comes to *salvation history*—the story of God's saving action made known in time and place—we are always on the lookout for those "magic moments" when divine reality is revealed in human terms. In such moments, what is always true for God suddenly becomes clear to us. We call these events *epiphanies*, occasions when God communicates the divine presence tangibly enough for us to grasp it. An epiphany is heaven breaking into time. It is Divine Revelation 101 for beginners, hard to miss and impossible to forget.

***

The Baptism of Jesus is such an occasion. The *Catechism of the Catholic Church* speaks of this event as the inauguration of Jesus' public ministry (see nos. 535–536). Little is known about the first thirty years of Jesus' life; he remains hidden like a seed in the ground, awaiting the hour of emergence. Then, as Hebrew prophecy had foretold, John springs first onto the public scene in anticipation of "the one who is to come." His message and his baptism are for repentance: the renouncing of sin and a change of heart. John's controversial and charismatic presence acts as a lure to draw sinners into the Light. John knows well that he is not the Light. He is only its primary witness.

John's ministry lures more than sinners, however. His stunning words and activity at the river are a catalyst for an epiphany like few others in history. Jesus is not a sinner, but he comes to the river to unite himself with the nature of sinners so as to share our death and restore us to new and fuller life. We may be surprised that the relationship between baptism and death is so keen. Jesus will later refer to the nearness of his Passion as "a baptism with which I must be baptized, and how great is my anguish until it is accomplished" (Luke 12:50). Through these words we come to appreciate how Jesus' acceptance of baptism is simultaneously an embrace of God's entire will from here to the cross. The Baptism of Jesus does not wash away any sin of his but rather opens the floodgates of his assent to carry the burden of sin to the limits of this world—and beyond.

As Saint Ambrose would later preach to the Church: "See where you are baptized, see where baptism comes from, if not from the cross of Christ, from his death! There is the whole mystery: He died for you."

***

A wonderful mystery is revealed here, but we have to be clear about what it is. Too often our focus on the revelation of Jesus withers into a morose interpretation of those words: "He died for you." Jesus is no masochist preferring the way of suffering to a happy life. Nor is God a monster pleased to crush the Just One with infirmity. There is no divine plot to cast God's Lamb onto the holocaust of human disobedience. The words "He died for you" show us that Jesus, one like us, is capable of making a choice for or against the will of God and that he chooses God utterly. We also see God's delight in the choice Jesus makes. God calls Jesus the "Beloved Son," that is, the One with the divine nature. What follows from Jesus' perfect choice is not the will of God alone; it also involves the will of human beings, as the Gospels make readily apparent. Jesus chose to say "yes," and people chose to put that "yes" to death.

***

The choice is now ours. By our baptism, we make Jesus' assent our own, becoming agents for the power of the Holy Spirit and members of the community of the Church. The symbolism of water here is significant. As Hebrew history tells us, the Flood in Noah's time and the parting of the Red Sea long ago revealed God's plan for salvation in the midst of the waters. Water was long the vehicle for religious purification. All these signs testify to the power of baptism to cleanse, save and deliver us.

Yet we cannot forget the warning in Saint Paul's words in Romans 6:3: "Are you unaware that we who are baptized into Christ Jesus were baptized into his death?" In baptism we are "buried" with Christ, dead to the empty promises of a world that is passing. We are dead to these things not because God is cruel but because Love has better things in mind for those who respond to this call. Those who enter the tomb with Christ will also learn the delight of rising to glory. Baptism is the ark that will take us there. Baptism is, as Jesus revealed to us, our first and most perfect *yes*. If we really want to know what time it is, we will find no better answer than this: It is time to understand that we too are God's delight.

The Second Luminous Mystery

The Miracle at Cana

In Cana of Galilee there was a wedding feast, and Jesus and his disciples had been invited. The mother of Jesus was also present. During the feasting, the wine ran out, and Jesus' mother approached him and said, "They have no more wine."

Jesus responded, "Woman, what concern is that to you, and to me? My hour has not yet come."

His mother went to the servants and advised them, "Do whatever he tells you." Standing nearby were six stone jars used for the Jewish purification rites. Each held twenty or thirty gallons. Jesus said to the servants, "Fill these jars with water." And when they were filled to the brim, Jesus told them, "Draw some out, and take it to the chief steward." So they took it.

When the chief steward tasted the water that had become wine, he did not know where it had come from. He called to the bridegroom and remarked, "Everyone serves the good wine first and then the inferior wine after the guests have had their fill! But you have kept the good wine until now." Jesus performed the first of his signs in Cana of Galilee, and so revealed his glory. And his disciples believed in him.

—the Gospel of John

Obedience has had an ambivalent reputation since the 1960s, when questioning authority came into vogue. People who followed rules and leaders unreflectively were scorned as fools. "My country, right or wrong" was an idea that came under scrutiny, as did any sort of knee-jerk allegiance to Church or creed. Social norms about law and order were challenged by those who thought leaders should earn the right to lead by demonstrating the sound-ness of their vision. Whether the issue was war, sexual mores, race relations, gender roles or economic justice, one thing was clear: People were waking up to the idea of personal accountability; they were no longer satisfied with being treated as sheep.

Fortunately, we are rid of the old model of obedience: Tuck your head and do what you are told. This model, after all, was not true to the root meaning of the word, which is "attentive listening." *Obedient* people are not those who follow a corporate decree with-out choosing for themselves or thinking critically. Obedient peo-ple first hear and savor, then act upon what they have come to un-derstand. This is how the prophets of old came to know God's word. This is how sinners, down through the centuries, have grown into saints.

***

Mary's obedience has been lauded as one of her greatest virtues. But she did not simply "hear the word of God and keep it." She also taught others to do the same. In this sense she embraced an early role as not only a model for discipleship but as a director of disciples. Mary of Nazareth could hardly be mistaken for a "sheep." Ever watchful for a chance to bring God's will into being, she noticed the gradual reduction of wine at the wedding and saw in it a unique opportunity.

What did Mary see? Pious commentators have sometimes read this event as an example of Mary's charity in worrying about the newlyweds and their shame in not being able to accommodate their guests. But would a woman so uniquely in tune with the movement of the Holy Spirit be concerned about a little loss of face? Would Mary commandeer the power inherent in her Son over a trifle?

Recent scholars have highlighted Mary's discernment in this event. First, she brought the matter to Jesus' attention because she perceived a teachable moment for the disciples. As Scripture notes, after the first sign at Cana the disciples believed in Jesus— which indicates they weren't at all convinced until that time. Second, Mary exercised her maternal role in giving birth to Jesus' public ministry by prodding him to act. This miracle, related only in John's Gospel, replaces both the narrative of Jesus' birth and his Baptism. John the Evangelist sought to draw a parallel between the physical role Mary played as Christ-bearer with the spiritual role she accepted as Jesus' first teacher. Mary did not give birth only to Jesus of Nazareth but also to Emmanuel, who is God-With-Us. Just as a mother knows when the time to give birth has arrived, so Mary instinctively knew when the time was ripe for Jesus to be revealed as the one who acts with the authority of God.

***

Is this not a more dynamic and vigorous form of obedience than what many of us remember from our early years? Mary heard the Word of God because it lived in her. Even before God's Word resided in her physically and was knit to her flesh, she had contained it and expressed it in authentic obedience. She listened; she savored; she dwelled in the Word until she knew it. And then it came forth from her, as the child Jesus once came forth from her, yet ever remaining intimately part of her life.

As Mary listened and understood, so she taught her Son, just as later she undertook the instruction of others. We see it in her approach with the servants at the wedding. "Do whatever he tells you," she advises them. This is, of course, a condensed version of what Mary did herself, following the word of God with great fidelity and generosity even though it may have sounded quite mysterious to her. So the servants must have thought it strange to get her instruction, followed by the command of Jesus to fill the huge ceremonial jars—long past their ritual usefulness on this occasion. Yet those who do not vainly question true authority will be the recipients of signs and wonders, as on that extraordinary day in Cana.

***

Genuine obedience has always been more than paying lip service to a governing body or a set of rules. Over and over throughout Israel's history, the people of God declared, "Everything the Lord has said, we will heed and do." And then they didn't. But we see in Mary what happens when that tendency is reversed and the believer embraces the will of God with total confidence. Mary the obedient becomes Mary the teacher. The Mother of Jesus becomes the initiator of his whole ministry. "Do whatever he tells you" remains the best wisdom for disciples like ourselves to take to heart. God still desires to work in our world, but we, like Mary, must embrace the responsibility to prepare the way.

The Third Luminous Mystery

The Proclamation of the Kingdom

After the arrest of John, Jesus withdrew to Galilee, leaving Nazareth and making his home in Capernaum by the sea. This was to fulfill what the prophet Isaiah had declared:

Land of Zebulun, land of Naphtali,
on the road by the sea, across the Jordan,
Galilee of the Gentiles—
the people who have walked in darkness
have seen a great light,
and for those who sat in the shadow of death
a great light has dawned.

From that time on, Jesus took up the message, "The time is fulfilled, and the kingdom of God has come near. Repent, and believe in the good news!"
—*the Gospels of Matthew and Mark*

We used to hear a lot about heaven. (Although we heard more, perhaps, about hell, heaven's alternative retirement community.) But talk of the afterlife in general is down, in part because the world we live in is so compelling. People of every generation have been consumed more with the tangible present than the shadowy never-never land of life after death. Apart from scattered reports about bright lights and lost relatives from those who have had near-death experiences, what do we really know about what comes next? And since we have no clear picture of what awaits us, what is there to talk about?

Meanwhile, there is much to say about the reality we face in the here and now. Friends and relatives who are still among us are in trouble. Bills need to be paid; repairs need to be done. Plans are in the works for the next vacation, the upcoming school year, the new job or the old car. Before we step one foot on the floor in the morning, our thoughts are revving up for the day ahead—its meetings, tasks, responsibilities and meals. In the third millennium it is rare to hear, even from small children, the words that used to haunt vast and motionless summers: "I have nothing to do!"

So when some prophet comes along and starts talking about the hereafter, we are inclined to be dismissive. What's that about and why should we care? The end of the world may be near, but we've all got lots to accomplish between now and then. Heaven has been reduced in our imaginations to a white cloud somewhere, populated by angels with harps. It is a place where lost relatives are stored until the apocalypse, a play land of saints and other unrealities. In effect, heaven is a place we have no time to contemplate between now and soccer practice. God's in his heaven, we say. It's another way of saying that heaven is a place for God, not for the likes of us.

All of this is useful to consider when we turn to Jesus' proclamation about the reign or kingdom of God. Frankly, Jesus is no more interested in pie-in-the-sky-when-you-die than we are. Jesus didn't come to announce that someday—a long, long time from now—you might go to heaven, if you are found worthy enough. Rather, Jesus spoke with an urgency that suggests we ought to be concerned right now: "The time is fulfilled, and the reign of God is near. Repent and believe the good news" (Mark 1:15).

***

The reign is near—or far? We sense the tension in the question. The reason we don't speak of heaven much is because, if we can get past mortal skepticism to entertain the idea at all, we presume it must be in a faraway place and time. Distant in place, for sure; this world has some really nice qualities and we would be loath to leave it, but we know it's not heaven. So heaven is someplace decidedly "other." Likewise, we assume heaven is far removed from us in time, like our death. No matter how old we are, most of us are still hoping for a cushion of time between now and the hour of our death. Even as we pray the rosary, asking Mary to be mindful of us now and in that hour, we anticipate that those are two very *different* hours. Someday, we vaguely acknowledge, "now" and "death" will be encompassed in the same hour. But not now, dear Lord. And not soon.

Yet Jesus says the kingdom is near and that the time is fulfilled. In place and in time, then, we seem to have lost the cushion of— let's say it—the security we hope to have between heaven and us, however pleasant it is reputed to be. The sticking point, we admit, is that we have to die to get there. Although it is rumored that death has no sting, we're not entirely convinced. We may have even watched how it stung a few of our loved ones on their way out of mortal life. Few of us are anxious to find out for ourselves.

***

Jesus provides a ready answer to our concerns—and of course, it isn't the answer we were hoping for. As a priest friend of mine likes to say, "Don't wait to die to go to heaven! Choose heaven right now and share its joy."

Jesus takes that idea one step further. He says: Don't wait till the end of your life to die; die to sin right now and live in the kingdom today. This is the essence of the antique word *repent*. We die to sin. We turn and face a new direction. We change and become less attached to the stuff of this world, more enamored of the kingdom that is coming, like a drumbeat, ever closer to us. If we listen, we can almost perceive its rhythm in our blood.

Human as we are, however, we are trapped at the corner of Space and Time, at the intersection of Here and Now, and it is hard to see anything beyond us. Jesus knew and proclaimed the kingdom, not quite here and not exactly there—but *coming*, in motion, headed this way. If he was talking about heaven, it's not the heaven we are used to, the static and faraway eternal rest home. That heaven is a place we have to go *to*, through the doorway of death.

The kingdom Jesus talked about is coming *in our direction.* All we have to do is turn around and be suffused with it. Jesus said the kingdom we are waiting for is actually within us. In the light of such an extraordinary reality, the safety net of time and space is discarded altogether. If the kingdom is within us, like a life, then perhaps it is up to us to participate in its birth. So we pray, with eyes wide open, *Thy kingdom come!*

The Fourth Luminous Mystery

The Transfiguration of Jesus

Jesus took with him Peter, James, and John and went up on the mountain to pray. While he was at prayer, the appearance of his face changed. His clothes became dazzling white. As the disciples watched in amazement, suddenly they saw two men, Moses and Elijah, talking to Jesus. They appeared in glory and were speaking about his departure, which he was about to accomplish at Jerusalem. Now Peter and his companions were weighed down with sleep; but because they remained awake they saw the glory of Jesus and the two who stood with him.

Just as the visitation was ending, Peter said to Jesus, "Master, it is good for us to be here! Let us make three tents: one for you, one for Moses, and one for Elijah." He hardly knew what he was saying. And as he spoke, a cloud came and overshadowed them; and they were terrified as they entered the cloud. Then came a voice from the cloud that proclaimed, "This is my Son, my chosen! Listen to him!"

—the Gospel of Luke

Have you ever felt that you were in the right place at the right time? Maybe you slipped onto the train with seconds to spare. Perhaps you were the one who made the championship catch or helped a friend in need at a place you went to by mistake. Sometimes we fall into employment opportunities, or even into love, just because we happened to be standing there. We know it had nothing to do with our abilities or even our choices. By the grace of God, we were there!

Peter expresses that same astonishment, perception and gratitude when he and the others stumble into an encounter with the transfigured Lord. "How good it is for us to be here" (Mark 9:5; Matthew 17:4; Luke 9:33). Because Peter knows this experience is pure gift, he wants to hang onto its grace as long as possible. Finding himself inexplicably the recipient of wonder, he can be forgiven for wanting it to last.

***

The Transfiguration is a curious sort of miracle. For the most part, nothing happens. No one is cured, nothing is multiplied, demons are not chased away, and the laws of nature are not spectacularly broken—unless you count the suspension of the separation between the living and the dead, that is. But once it's over, nothing much appears to have changed.

The disciples, God bless their souls, are no different. On their way down the mountain, they furtively discuss the meaning of this event. But it leaves no lasting impression on them. If they had understood anything they had seen, they would have remained faithful all the way to the cross.

So what did the Transfiguration accomplish? Was it some sort of divine pep talk for Jesus' own benefit? Did Moses and Elijah appear for an afternoon of theological discussion about what was to transpire in Jerusalem? Did the voice from heaven speak to call Jesus "Beloved" one more time before the whole ministry came crashing down around him? What kind of cameo of grace are we to see in that hour on Mount Tabor? Maybe in the word *cameo* we may seek understanding—how in the small frame of an instant the greatness of a person can be brought into sharp relief.

***

The Transfiguration is a kind of miracle of the eyes; that is, a miraculous way of seeing and perceiving. It's a glimpse, a lifting of the veil, a revelation in the finest sense. It was not intended to be permanent or prolonged, just a "moment of truth" in which one comes to understand something that has always been true but is fully appreciated only in this new encounter. We can speculate on what the Transfiguration meant for Jesus or for Peter, James and John, but the only really important question is: What does it mean for us? What do we see when we contemplate that illuminated face of Jesus?

In *Rosarium Virginis Mariae*, Pope John Paul II spoke of this event as an icon for Christian contemplation (see no. 9). If we choose to linger with the mystery for a while, as Peter expressed the desire to do, its beauty may entrance us. We may gradually begin to recognize how the power of the Transfiguration operates all the time amid our day-to-day experiences, in the celebrations and sufferings of life. As Peter learned much later, what he saw on Mount Tabor that day was always true of the One he followed.

***

We too might discover the face of beauty and truth in ordinary places, in strangers, in simple rituals, if we open ourselves to this way of seeing. The path to attaining this sort of miracle of the eyes is through the practice of contemplation. As Jesus told Philip, who was ambitious to see the face of God: "Philip, if you have seen me, you have seen the Father" (John 14:9). Just as in a cameo performance, when a great actor walks on stage for just a moment, the full glory of God was on display for a mere instant on Mount Tabor. But it is also constantly on view for those who perceive who Jesus is through his life of teaching and healing, his command over nature and demons alike. The hidden revelation of God, we might say, resides in the everyday Jesus. So if we pay close attention to the ordinary, we just might see some remarkable transfigurations ourselves.

Can we see the Madonna in the pregnant teenager, or the crucified Christ in the homeless man on the street? Is the sacred available to us in secular moments or do we look for holiness exclusively in the faces of plaster saints and in the goings-on at church? Do we seek God only on the mountaintop or are we willing to find the divine on our way to the bottom? Is glory accessible to us in beautiful scenes alone or do we dare to look at misery until we pierce the veil and see what God sees in humble places?

The holy face of Christ was transfigured, once by the blinding light on Mount Tabor and once by the anguish of the cross. After the Resurrection, Jesus' appearance was so changed that even his friends did not know him.

Would we who count ourselves among the friends of Christ recognize him if we saw his face today?

The Fifth Luminous Mystery

The Sacrament of the Eucharist

> Before the festival of the Passover, Jesus knew his hour had come to depart from this world and go to the Father. Having loved his own who were in the world, he loved them to the end. That evening Jesus took his place with the twelve at table. And while they were eating, Jesus took a loaf of bread. After blessing it, he broke it, gave it to the disciples and said, "Take. Eat. This is my body." Then he took the cup filled with wine, and after giving thanks he gave it to them, saying, "Drink from it, all of you. For this is my blood of the covenant, which is poured out for many, for the forgiveness of sin. Do this in remembrance of me."
>
> —*the Gospels of Matthew, Luke, and John*

Spiritual writer Anthony de Mello told the story of how God sent the angels to travel the earth to report on the circumstance of humankind. They returned one by one with the same message: "Everywhere on earth, the people are hungry." So God made an astounding decision: "Then I will come to them as food."

This is the clearest and shortest theology of the Eucharist we may find. Because we are hungry, God elects to feed us. Because we are needy, God supplies what we lack. Volumes have been written about the precise significance and substance of the sacrament we celebrate with bread and wine. But as Saint Thomas Aquinas, writer of some of those tomes, was first to admit, any theory of the Eucharist is dust and ashes compared to the vital experience of actually receiving the life of Christ within us.

***

Hunger is one of the readiest windows through which we can

view and come to appreciate this sacrament. As theologian Monika Hellwig has noted, most people who have ever lived on this planet, including the majority who live here right now, have known hunger as their fundamental human experience. As citizens of the First World, we forget how common a reality the threat of hunger is. We speak of being "starved to death" even as we sit in a restaurant awaiting an ample meal. But what of those whose stomachs wrench with a need that was not satisfied yesterday and won't be satisfied again today? Real physical hunger is something that is beyond our scope, no matter how hungry we think we are. So we are tempted to spiritualize the meaning of the meal Jesus prepares for us, since we have no appreciation of our real need.

Yet Mother Teresa saw in our land of privilege the worst poverty she had ever imagined. What did she mean, coming from the streets of Calcutta and calling America the land of the truly poor? Certainly our need is not physical. We are groaning with material excess, a country of the obese in the land of the super-sized snack and the overstuffed chair. To judge from our stores and catalogues, the most common crisis in America is where and how to store all our stuff. Should we reorganize our closets, add a shed to the yard, rent a space downtown or just get a bigger house? At the same time, we know we are the land of the depressed and the anxious, the greedy and the lonely. Somehow, despite all we have and all we consume, we cannot fill the void that seems to be gaining on us. Our great hunger may not be physical, but it is gnawing us to pieces all the same.

***

And so Jesus sets a place at the table even for those of us who are in no apparent need of food. Our swollen need is to learn mercy, and we need to learn it from the One whose mercy led to the cross. Right before he goes to his death, in full knowledge of what is coming, Jesus shares a meal with his friends. Is this like the final supper of a man facing execution, a last comfort before the end? If it is, the comfort is for those invited to the meal, not for

Jesus. The one who gave himself in every act of proclamation, charity, healing and teaching now shows his mercy in bread and wine, just as he is about to demonstrate it more acutely at Golgotha. If we can grasp *the absolute necessity of compassion* in the fellowship of Christ, then we will go a long way in appropriating the meaning of Eucharist into our daily lives.

John's Gospel bypasses the symbol of the meal in favor of the rich example of the washing of the feet. This later gospel writer reflects on the dual command of Jesus on that last evening: not simply to take in, but to give out. If we believe that the Eucharist is a spiritual richness given to us for our personal benefit, we have missed its meaning by a mile. You must do as I have done, Jesus instructs the disciples. As I have fed you, so you must feed others. This call to service is essential to true and complete Eucharist.

***

One of the dangers of living in a society not physically aware of its need is that we fall asleep to the reality of the needs of others. We begin to dream that sacraments are for worthy people who have earned them by refraining from sin, like a meal set for the righteous. So our Eucharist begins and ends with us, and we remain profanely bloated with it. Putting aside our delusion of righteousness for a moment, how truly incapacitated is the grace we have been offered, paralyzed in transit by our lack of generosity. If we take and eat and do not share—if we bless and break and do not distribute—then we may find ourselves choking on our own injustice. Jesus' teaching on judgment is clear: What we do for the least of our sisters and brothers we do for him. By extension, what we withhold from the rest of the human family in need we refuse to the very person of Christ.

Armed with this understanding, we come to the table in great need of being emptied, unburdened, relieved of our excess, hopeful that the Lord of Mercy will show us compassion—and teach us that compassion for the sake of others. For the blood of Christ was poured out for many, as he told us plainly, not just for us.

The Sorrowful
Mysteries

The First Sorrowful Mystery

The Agony in the Garden

> Jesus went with them to a place called Gethsemane and said to his disciples, "Sit here while I go over there and pray." He took with him Peter and the two sons of Zebedee, and he began to be distressed and agitated. Then he said to them, "I am deeply grieved, even to death; remain here and stay awake with me." Going on a little farther, he threw himself on the ground and prayed, "My Father, if it is possible, let this cup pass away from me; yet not what I will, but your will be done." Then he came back to the disciples and found them asleep, and he said to Peter, "So, could you not stay awake with me one hour? Stay awake and pray that you may not come into the time of trial; the spirit is willing, but the flesh is weak."
>
> *—the Gospel of Matthew*

Betrayal comes in all sizes, and it is a regular part of our experience. Although we hope for nothing less than loyalty and support from those who know us, which of us has not felt the disappointment of being denied or abandoned in an hour of need?

The litany of letdown begins early. Small playground reversals are common. For example, your best buddy sides with the in-crowd and the earthquake of betrayal rumbles through your world. But likely this is not your first experience of rejection. Your parents may have withheld something vital to your sense of security or need for approval, or perhaps a sibling has blamed you for what he or she knows was not your fault. The net of betrayal is cast farther and wider as the years progress, and we begin to sense the presence of it in school, on the job, in politics and in the acute space of intimate relationships.

Perhaps the most tender trespasses come to us from the world of religion, where we least expect a traitor to reside. If we are shocked by what religious leaders, global or local, have done with our trust, then maybe we ought to pay closer attention to the story of Jesus. Those who delivered him to the Romans or ran from him in the critical hour were all religious people. His enemies were upstanding leaders of the assembly, versed in Scripture and keepers of the moral code. Those who sought his death weren't foreigners and pagans, but rather citizens of his own country and fellow Jews. The danger to Jesus never came from without. It reared its head deep within his special corps of religious friends. In the end, it wasn't some impersonal devil that brought Jesus to the cross. It was the combined weakness and malice of some of the most righteous people in the land.

***

The seed of desertion is evident in the Garden of Gethsemane. If the disciples had heard anything at dinner, it was that Jesus was closing shop on his teaching ministry. He even gave them something to remember him by: a Eucharist to celebrate for ages to come. But these followers, his closest friends and longtime students, seem strangely indifferent to this event, ignorant of its pathos. Despite the fact that Jesus had been talking about his imminent death for many weeks, they close their eyes to his anxiety. And when he asks three of his dearest companions to pray with him in his hour of obvious anguish, they fall asleep instead. His isolation is complete. Jesus has no one willing to share the last mile of his struggle.

Luke, keenly aware of the trauma of this desertion, supplies Jesus a comforting angel for companionship. But the two earlier accounts, in Mark and Matthew, show us Jesus prostrate on the ground, in agony and alone as he faces the approaching hour of suffering. This is the essence of betrayal: not that there is no one present to offer support but that the ones who ought to be there have chosen not to be.

If the disciples are not willing to give an hour to their friend in prayer, will they be more eager to give their testimony in the trial and execution to follow? Clearly not. If they had prayed to withstand the test to come, as Jesus sorrowfully informs them, they might have held fast against the temptation to run and hide. But they are weak, and weakness leads reflexively to self-preservation. They have not developed the discipline necessary to steel the will in favor of the truth when it comes at the expense of the self.

***

As humans subject to the cruelty of betrayal, we know something of Jesus' experience in his final hour. But if we are honest, we admit that we are more familiar with the role of the traitor. We surrender our principles when an opportunity comes along that benefits those who are morally more "flexible." We betray our faith when laziness tempts us to neglect or deny our Christian witness. We allow gossip about our friends to occur in our presence and may even add to the brew ourselves. We turn away from human suffering and pretend we do not see the face of Christ. We refuse our responsibility to stand up against injustice, violence and the oppression of groups or individuals. If we add up the litany of our traitorous acts, we might find cause for despair.

***

Jesus does not expend his energy making lists of offenses against him, however. He heartily prefers treating sin with forgiveness. He forgives those who do not know the consequence of what they are doing, even as they participate most deliberately in his crucifixion. He seeks out his wayward disciples directly after the Resurrection and offers them peace. He takes Peter, his denier, aside personally and welcomes his three-fold recommitment in love. We may regard ourselves as traitors to our faith—but Jesus calls us friends. We have only to decide which name will have the greater claim on who we are to become.

Contrition is the traditional virtue of this mystery of the rosary, and it is contrition that brings us to the full and sincere confession of our sin. When we acknowledge our desertions along the way of love, we put ourselves within the grasp of the grace necessary to regain that path. Jesus invites us to be his companions and to share his life with him. If we have departed from his company, there is no finer hour than the present to rejoin him.

The Second Sorrowful Mystery

The Scourging at the Pillar

Pilate, fearing the reaction of the crowds, asked them,
"What should I do with Jesus, who is called the Messiah?" All of them responded, "Let him be crucified!"
Then Pilate asked, "Why, what evil has he done?" But
they only shouted louder, "Let him be crucified!"

So when Pilate saw that he could do nothing, and
fearing that a riot would ensue, he took some water
and washed his hands before the crowds, saying, "I am
innocent of this man's blood; see to it yourselves."
Then the people cried, "His blood be on us and on our
children!" So Pilate released Barabbas for them; and
after having Jesus flogged he handed him over to be
crucified.

—the Gospel of Matthew

Dorothy Day cautioned her community of Catholic Workers
not to make distinctions between the "deserving" and the "undeserving" poor. She understood that we often judge others based on
whether they have contributed to their own suffering and mete
out our compassion accordingly. In this sense, we hold the poor
accountable the circumstance of their poverty. If they have caused
this situation by faulty choices and bad behaviors, well, then, why
should we feel sorry for them or be obliged to help?

The deeper truth of Christian compassion is that it has little to
do with how we feel. Compassion is a divinely inspired movement
from the depths of our being that calls us to respond according to
God's will with action and not mere pity. When Jesus experiences
compassion, he responds with teaching, healing or food. He never
stops to consider the worthiness of this leper or that blind person.
He does not mull over the virtue of the crowd before he feeds

them. In the exercise of her ministry, Dorothy Day found some of the disadvantaged people who came to her personally compelling and others positively repugnant. But she did not allow her emotions to govern her commitment to address their need.

Service to the poor is hard work. We don't like it because it puts us in touch with the seamy and vulnerable side of being human, including the unattractive and untouchable parts of ourselves. To insulate ourselves from the discomfort of contact with the disadvantaged, then, we set up barriers to a compassionate response. We create very exclusive conditions under which our compassion may be engaged: no addicts, for example, or no criminals; no one guilty of domestic violence or unruly speech and behavior; no folks unwilling to clean up their act, or those unprepared to get a job and manage their own affairs; no mental illness; no foreigners; no quitters; no one who does not accept the name of the Lord Jesus. When we are finished qualifying our compassion, we may find few left who deserve it. And that, we may discover, is a profound relief.

***

Determining the innocence of poor people before showing them mercy, however, is an unwieldy task. When we examine the relative guilt or innocence of humanity, we have to take into account the words of Saint Paul, who insisted that no one is free from sin and that all of us have fallen short of innocence. To be precise, under the law of "just deserts," we *all* deserve *condemnation* (see Romans 3:22–23). If compassion is to be reserved for the innocent, then no one will get it—not you and not me. Guilt is, therefore, an undesirable measuring stick to use against others, since we know that human judgment draws down divine judgment upon it.

We see the unlikely claim of personal innocence at work in the judgment rendered by Pilate. He washes his hands of the Jesus issue, disavowing all responsibility. Yet it is Pilate's cohort of soldiers that removes Jesus to the recesses of the governor's own palace to continue his maltreatment and weaken him for execution. It is under Pilate's authority that an execution lawfully takes place. For a man with clean hands, Pilate sure has plenty of friends to do his dirty work.

And so we "innocent" citizens often have our dirty work performed for us, allowing the state to execute criminals in our name, paying for wars that target civilians, benefiting from economic policies that oppress people in lands far away, keeping our borders secure by turning away desperate hopefuls who risk their lives to come here, accepting racist and sexist institutions without protest, remaining silent as our air and water and wilderness are ravaged for the sake of profit. The politics of poverty and injustice implicate everyone. Like Pilate, we may wash our hands, but it is trickier by far to cleanse our hearts.

***

Who is guiltier of the death of Jesus—the leaders who initially sought his life, the disciple whose lips betrayed him, the mob that dragged him from the garden, the friends who deserted him, the governor who did not use his authority to release him, the soldiers who scourged him, or the ones who drove in the nails? Was it Rome or Jerusalem that put Jesus to death? What criteria would we use to render such a judgment? Centuries of theology assert that Jesus died for *our* sins. Can we be less guilty than the people of his generation? The assessment of guilt becomes a shell game, as we manipulate culpability to suit our own interests. But if Jesus was truly and completely innocent, then no one's hands are clean enough to escape responsibility.

***

As the poets and activists remind us, Jesus is still being scourged in our midst. If we prefer to claim our innocence in this matter, there is plenty yet to do on his behalf. Jesus once told his disciples how to escape judgment: feed the hungry; give drink to the thirsty; clothe the naked; welcome the stranger; visit the sick and the imprisoned. When we show compassion to these little ones, we offer it to him.

We also can take a lesson from the notorious woman who dared wipe the feet of Jesus with her hair. Jesus said of her, "The one who loves much is forgiven much" (Luke 7:47). When we love extravagantly—not only the deserving but also those we are tempted to label as undeserving of our love—we may find ourselves standing on that holy ground that became the proving ground for modern saints like Dorothy Day. Any number of people could have stood up against the machinery of Jerusalem and Rome during the trial and execution of Jesus—but no one did. As Jesus is led away to be scourged in our midst daily, the matter is still open before us. Will we mock or praise him? Participate in the beating or struggle for his release? Cry out against the injustice or simply remain silent, carefully washing our hands?

The Third Sorrowful Mystery

The Crowning with Thorns

> Then the soldiers of the governor took Jesus into the governor's headquarters, and they stripped him and put a scarlet robe on him. After twisting some thorns into a crown, they placed it on his head. Putting a reed in his right hand, they knelt before him and mocked him, saying, "All hail, King of the Jews!"
>
> Once more Pilate went out and said to the people, "Look, I am bringing him out to you, to let you know that I find no case against him." So Jesus came out, wearing the crown of thorns and the cloak. And Pilate said to them, "Behold the man!"
>
> —*the Gospels of Matthew and John*

Kings were ever a part of the story of Jesus. Significantly, he was born of the house of David, the great king of Israel whose rule God promised would last forever. David had been anointed by God through the oil of his prophet. It was widely anticipated that the one who was to save Israel from the throes of her history would be another "anointed one" like David. It was up to God to send this "messiah," and all the nation could do was wait.

Jesus was conceived by the power of the Holy Spirit and was given the Father's endorsement at his baptism. But he did not receive the oil of royal anointing till the end of his life, when an unknown woman came and poured it on him. The Gospels report the scene variously. In Mark and Matthew, the woman anoints Jesus' head with oil. In Luke and John, a woman (identified in John as Mary, the sister of Martha and Lazarus) bathes and perfumes his feet. Jesus responds to this act of love and kindness as a sobering preparation for his burial. For perceiving the closeness of his death, Jesus acknowledges the woman's actions as inspired; but he does not say that her prophetic anointing marks his kingship. He leaves that up to his enemies to proclaim. And, remarkably, they do.

***

Jesus showed a certain reluctance to claim the title of *messiah*. When the demons shrieked his identity, he commanded them to be silent. When the disciples guessed at who he was, he ordered them to say nothing to anyone. When Pilate asked him directly, "Are you the King of the Jews?" Jesus neither confirmed nor denied it. Claiming kingship in a world of puppet kings such as Herod or self-crowned emperors such as Caesar did not express the magnitude of authority that resided in Jesus. Nor did the popular Jewish expectations of a messiah come close to the role Jesus intended to play. So when people talked about worldly power, Jesus claimed nothing for himself. The most he would reveal to Pilate is that his kingdom was not of this world.

Still, kingship was the identity forced on Jesus in his last hours. They dressed him in mock royal robes and crowned him with brambles. They put a reed scepter in his weakened hand and humiliated him with false homage. Many years earlier, according to one story, real kings of the East had bowed before him in genuine adoration. But even then, while his kingship was being duly honored, another king was plotting his death. Jesus always had an ambivalent relationship with the earthly side of royal authority. It is no wonder he put himself at a distance from it.

Yet Jesus died under the title "King of the Jews." It was inescapable, this designation, nailed as a charge against him and given as the cause for his execution. Earthly kingship had become, quite frankly, a crime of sorts, as mortal kings greedily plundered their country's wealth, broke God's laws and reaped the consequences for both themselves and their people. But Jesus never was guilty of earthly kingship. His reign exerted the opposite force— generous love and protection—and reaped a far different consequence—salvation offered freely to all.

***

The kingdom Jesus proclaimed is to be inherited by the meek. Perhaps it was tragically suitable for the crown of thorns to become the symbol of that kingdom. It makes perfect sense that the only person to acknowledge the authenticity of the suffering king was a criminal who hung on a cross next to Jesus. The man asked only: "Remember me when you come into your kingdom" (Luke 23:42). For this testimony of faith, Jesus granted this criminal a king's pardon, opening the joy of paradise to him that very day.

What do we ask of Christ the King? Do we come to him in the spirit of meekness, seeking forgiveness and remembrance, or do we offer him the mockery of superficial allegiance, making religion a "Sunday front" for business as usual? Do we regard divine kingship as one more authority to be circumvented, as we do freeway cops, the IRS, family expectations and social conventions? Is the sovereignty of Jesus as meaningless to us as that of mortal kings, or do we view his power as commanding not only our allegiance but also our hearts?

***

Behold the man who is also the King of Kings! The meek know how to respond to such majesty. The proud, however, have no regard for authority outside of themselves. Americans are peculiarly susceptible to this kind of outlaw stance in response to power. We don't kneel, and we prefer not to bow. Being a mighty nation, we forget that the mightiest power ever to walk the earth chose to use its authority at the service of the weakest. The King of Kings mounted a throne that was coarse and deadly for the sake of those imperiled by the finality of death. Prophecy tells us that the Servant of God "opened not his mouth" but accepted suffering meek as a lamb. We who multiply our boasts before the world can only wonder at such silence. Majesty is known in the dignity of restraint.

It is hard for us to see that all First World citizens walk this earth with the authority of kings, our footsteps shaking the realm of the poor in whatever decisions we make. In light of this, the virtue of meekness is not simply an admirable spiritual practice but a matter of life or death for those who pay the consequences of our influence. We are forewarned that our authority, vast as it is, is merely of this world. The One whose kingdom is not here is the true source of all power, and it is to his name that every creature—human and angelic alike—must bow.

The Fourth Sorrowful Mystery

The Carrying of the Cross

They led him away to be crucified. And as they went out they compelled a passerby, who was coming in from the country, to carry his cross. It was Simon of Cyrene, the father of Alexander and Rufus. A great number of the people followed him, and among them were women who were beating their breasts and wailing for him. But Jesus turned to them and said, "Daughters of Jerusalem, do not weep for me, but weep for yourselves and for your children. For the days are surely coming when they will say, 'Blessed are the barren, and the wombs that never bore, and the breasts that never nursed.' Then they will begin to say to the mountains, 'Fall on us,' and to the hills, 'Cover us.' For if they do this when the wood is green, what will happen when it is dry?"

—*the Gospels of Mark and Luke*

When the time for dying comes, those affected by the loss react in quite different ways. Some attend the bedside or the hospital room of the sufferer with great fidelity and charity. Others absent themselves, not able to bear even the mention of imminent death. Certain individuals make themselves helpful out of guilt or leaden obligation. Others embrace the burden with easy hearts, eager to lighten the load and exercise their love. People will weep, rage, tell fond stories or bitter ones, and some will register no expression whatsoever. How we come before the death of others reveals a great deal about our own character and our grasp of the reality of human mortality. How we deal with our own dying is more revealing still.

The reaction of others to the imminent death of Jesus was highly complicated by the fact that he wasn't just dying—he was being killed. An execution isn't the same as expiring from illness or old age or an accident. As traumatic as the loss of a loved one is under any circumstance, watching one murdered in a highly public spectacle is many times more paralyzing. The particulars of crucifixion made it that much worse. It was by design a humiliating end, intended for slaves and social villains. It was meant to shame, involving exposure of the body along an open road, so that all who passed by could view the infamy and hurl an insult or two. Death by crucifixion set an example for moral, upstanding folk. You might take the kids to Golgotha to learn a lesson: "See? This is what happens when you live a bad life."

No one could have guessed that crucifixion was about to be translated into a sign of ultimate goodness and glory. Christian parents would hereafter bring their children before the cross and say: "See? This is what God was willing to do for love of us."

***

The way of the cross has become much more than a way of dying. It has spawned a devotion all its own, instructing us in a way of living. Within the Stations of the Cross, as they have become known, we focus on the "stations," those freeze-frame stops along the Good Friday road, unpacking each final lesson Jesus was teaching. We might also remember that the proper term for this devotion is *The Way of the Cross*, with its emphasis not on stopping but on pilgrimage. The journey toward the tomb teaches us well, precisely because we are all presently taking that journey. The Way of the Cross, in one form or another, is everyone's way. That's why Jesus, in his great mercy, was moved to take it ahead of us.

***

Simon of Cyrene, as several of the Gospels make clear, was forced to assist Jesus on that journey. Mark adds that Simon was the father of Alexander and Rufus, who would later become willing disciples of the Way through baptism. We like to think their father learned something that day to compel his heart, just as the soldiers compelled his physical strength. Did Simon's experience on the road shape the response that would result in his sons taking that journey for themselves?

Luke's Gospel focuses on the women who walked that road with Jesus. They cannot lighten his burden, but they grieve it with him in lament and companionship. Jesus offers them (and us) a practical suggestion: to share his sorrow in mortal solidarity as humans who are all subject to suffering and death. The proper focus of our twenty-first-century devotion to the carrying of the cross is not sentimental reflection on what it was like for Jesus to accept this death but what the meaning of our own deaths will be.

***

A third story of encounter enters the devotional vocabulary of the Way of the Cross: the tale of Veronica. Her appearance is not recorded in Scripture, but she is represented in tradition as the woman who braves the wrath of the soldiers by offering Jesus her veil to wipe the blood from his face. Isaiah had written about the suffering servant whose face was ruined by torment and horrible to behold. That face draws Veronica's fascination and compassion. Wordlessly, Veronica breaks through the guards to offer a moment's comfort to the One who looks upon the world with such great mercy. For her courage, we are told, she is rewarded with an everlasting image of that holy face.

***

How do we undertake our own Way of the Cross? Do we accept our sufferings under duress? Do we turn our unexpected and conscripted service into a life of discipleship? Do we recognize the pain of others as our own pain, because it is first of all the suffering of Christ, of whose Body we are a part? Can we find the courage to reveal the compassion of Christ, even in places where it is unwelcome and perhaps dangerous?

The way in which we undertake this journey shapes how it will end. The road has many surprises along the way, yet each mile is connected to the other, and all contribute to the person we are becoming, step by step. If we stay close to Jesus on his sorrowful journey, we may find it easier to walk others home along this well-worn route. And when it comes time for us to walk that final mile, we may find ourselves in very good company.

The Fifth Sorrowful Mystery

The Crucifixion and Death of Jesus

It was now about noon, and darkness came over the whole land until three in the afternoon while the sun's light failed. Standing near the cross of Jesus were his mother and his mother's sister, Mary, the wife of Clopas, and Mary Magdalene. When Jesus saw his mother and the disciple whom he loved standing beside her, he said to his mother, "Woman, here is your son." Then he said to the disciple, "Here is your mother." And from that hour the disciple took her into his own home.

After this, when Jesus knew that all was now finished, he said (in order to fulfill the Scripture), "I am thirsty." A jar of sour wine stood nearby, so they put a sponge full of wine on a branch of hyssop and held it to his mouth. When Jesus had received the wine, he said, "It is finished." Then he bowed his head and gave up his spirit.

At that moment, the curtain of the temple was torn in two, from top to bottom. The earth shook, and the rocks were split. The tombs were also opened, and many bodies of the saints who had fallen asleep were raised. After his resurrection they came out of the tombs and entered the holy city and appeared to many.

—*the Gospels of Matthew, Luke and John*

Nothing happens in isolation, neither in life nor in death. We are always aware of a thick sense of context affecting everything we do: the clock ticking on the wall, the way the sun falls in the room, the chill in the air, the sound of a far-off voice. The things that happen to us are influenced by the strong associations of memory. A girl's smile reminds us of another smile long ago. A young man resembles his father. This generation's war, sadly, recalls too many just like it.

Even our hopes or fears regarding the future tend to color our present experience and become part of its inevitable context. Perhaps this illness will be the final one. Maybe a new job will lead to financial security. Perhaps a vacation could be the turning point that will save our marriage.

Because it is impossible to separate a single event from everything that surrounds it in time and place, we embrace our lives as a helix of meaning—a long, complex and interdependent strand of experience. Each piece is linked to the next. Every new face becomes part of the old story and draws its role in response to the whole. Will this person be a hero, a villain, part of the problem or part of the solution? Will our situation get better or worse from here? Is this bend in the road a beginning or is the story winding down to its conclusion? Nothing happens, we come to realize, out of the blue. Each episode has its root and flower descending and ascending in what was, is and will be. Call it luck, grace, fate or timing: What comes to us bears a message we interpret through the lens of a complete life perspective.

***

The crucifixion of Jesus occurred on a typical Friday in first-century Jerusalem. Dogs barked, children played, men went to their shops and women to their tasks. It was during the Feast of Passover, and the Sabbath was hours away, so there was much preparation in the air. A secret council of elders had been held in the night, and a trial by the governor later that morning had condemned an innocent man to death. Three criminals were being crucified outside of town at noon that day. Ah, well. Life goes on for the rest of us.

Of course, many had heard of Jesus, and some would regret that he was among those being executed. Others who championed the keeping of the peace would be relieved. Some citizens of both camps would take off work to follow the procession out of town and watch with fascination or horror as the deed was done. These things were morbid, but they couldn't be helped.

For those who followed Jesus and loved him, the day was one of tragedy and incomprehensibility. They wept, fell on their knees, held one another and prayed for the mountains to fall on them or their enemies. Some were in hiding. Others witnessed the immensity of the injustice from beginning to end. Jesus' own Mother saw her Son put to death by coldly rational men right before her eyes. How she was able to add this to the contents of her heart is known only to parents who have suffered the deaths of their children. The child whose birth was announced by God's angel was crucified in God's inexplicable silence.

Meanwhile, the sky darkened, the Temple was violated, the earth quaked and the dead were awakened. All around this little scene of chaos and grief, creation groaned aloud at the death of God's Beloved.

***

Jesus, too, had a response to the drama of which he was the center. He saw it as the end, not only of his life but of the mission he had come to fulfill and the divine work he had set out to accomplish. Because he was deeply aware of his obligation to the past, Jesus gave his Mother into the care of a friend. Because Jesus also was conscious of his obligation to the future, he gave his friend a mother who would be strong and faithful until the hour of death. His Mother had a new home; the Church had a new Mother. And then finally, responsible only to the present hour, Jesus fulfilled the word of the prophets. Answering only to God's will, he laid down his life.

***

When we suffer, the pain may become so great that it fills our perception and isolates us from everything but its own inescapable presence. But loneliness is now and ever will be the devil's lie.

God's silence is never the same as absence or disregard. We are accompanied through every misery, even to the hour of our death, by a Love so great that its passing set the earth trembling and the dead rose from their sleep in response to it. We trust the stories of the past. We trust the promise to come. But mostly, we trust the present hour, where Jesus said he would always be found, even to the end of time.

The Glorious Mysteries

The First Glorious Mystery

The Resurrection

At daybreak on the first day of the week, the women who had accompanied Jesus from Galilee took the spices they had prepared and went to the tomb. They found the stone rolled away, but when they entered they did not find the body of the Lord. As they puzzled over this, two men in dazzling garments appeared to them. Terrified, they bowed their faces to the ground. The dazzling strangers said, "Why do you seek the living among the dead? He is not here. He has been raised. Remember what he told you back in Galilee, that the Son of Man must be handed over to sinners and be crucified and rise on the third day." They did remember his words. Then they left the tomb and announced all these things to the eleven and to the others. The women were Mary Magdalene, Joanna, and Mary, the mother of James; the others who accompanied them also told this to the apostles.

—the Gospel of Luke

As a religious symbol, the empty tomb is a marvel. It's an unanticipated absence, a sign of cool inconsistency with the laws of nature, a divine surprise that has no equal in the human experience. Death is so predictably final that we have a saying: "The only sure things in life are death and taxes." But after the Resurrection, it would appear that we can count only on taxes!

The Christian belief that Jesus did not stay dead changes everything for those who embrace it. If the crucifixion had ended in a somber burial and the remembrance of a heroic man and his noble teachings, we'd have on our hands something along the lines of a Greek tragedy—beautiful and instructive. But the story of Jesus is not a tragedy. Rather, it is *gospel*—that is, good news, a message to be spread far and wide. The gospel requires *apostles,* people sent to bear this news to those who haven't heard it. Apostles are given the *Spirit,* to fill them with the gifts necessary to carry out their mission. And so fortified, they encourage the *Church,* which becomes the soil generating new apostles for each successive generation until the end of the ages.

All of this—the gospel, the apostles, the Spirit and the Church—emerges from the empty tomb. What a curious place to engender such hope. What a vacant site to be the repository of so much wonder.

***

The Resurrection of Jesus is the central tenet of Christian faith. Yet for being such a pivotal event it is wrapped in complete mystery. No one saw it happen; we have no report of how it might have taken place. If Jesus explained the mechanics of it to his rapt disciples in the upper room, they did not share the details with us. The only symbol left to us of this faith-making event is the empty tomb—an anticlimactic sign if ever there was one. That empty tomb mutely yawns before us, keeping its secrets. It tells us nothing of what it once contained, only what it could no longer hold.

The tomb, in all its mystery, is the first and most consistent witness of Easter. In the gospel accounts of this historic morning, various actors come and go. Women (always including Mary Magdalene and sometimes only her) find the tomb in its interrupted state. In one version, Peter and another disciple come by to inspect its contents. Who knows how many soldiers of Pilate or emissaries of the High Priest tramp through the tomb before the day is over, furious at this unexpected development.

The reports of what people see in all this emptiness vary as well. Some are frightened and run away. Some walk around, look at the neatly piled burial cloths, and are mystified. Some "see and believe," even though they "do not yet understand." Some encounter angels with helpful explanations or commanding messages. In one Easter story, Mary Magdalene even meets the newly resurrected Lord but mistakes him for a gardener. This "empty" tomb, we come to understand, is quite full of surprises.

***

What we see in the open tomb, needless to say, is the linchpin of our faith as well. In its maw, this legendary space contains all of Christianity to come. Yet it takes the eyes of faith to see something in the apparent nothingness of the tomb. From Easter to Easter, as the seasons of our lives engage and challenge us in new ways, we return to this spot, look in and experience a variety of perceptions of the space. Some years the tomb really is empty and deserted to us, and we wonder where God has gone and whether our faith has been a cheat. Sometimes we encounter real Presence and feel that we too "have seen the Lord!" At times we feel confused by this event: What does this sign mean and does it have more than mere historical significance for us? At other times we feel more hope than faith: If only the Resurrection could be true and our dear ones are waiting for us somewhere.

The traditional virtue attached to this mystery is faith, because faith alone will lead us when heart and hope may fail. *Thinking* about the Resurrection brings us to theology. Only *trusting* in it can make us confident enough to live our dying, as Christians have a singular vocation to do.

***

We do not come to the empty tomb alone, however. The holy women have been here ahead of us, as well as the male disciples, a few angels, and doubtless more than a few unbelievers. We come to this place on the heels of centuries of Christians and would-be Christians and non-Christians and anti-Christians who peered in and walked around a bit before making up their minds and hearts about this curious evidence. To what does it testify? And what does it mean? If by the grace of God Jesus has thwarted death and the devil—well, good for him. But if he has moved the stone, so to speak, to clear a way for the rest of us to follow, then this is an even more remarkable story. If death has lost its sting and the devil his best punch, then we have cause for rejoicing at decibels that will rattle the heavens. A chorus of Alleluias is only the beginning.

The Resurrection is a historical event but also a dynamic assertion that redefines everything. If death has lost its finality, then nothing is as certain as it once was. Perhaps the empty tomb is packed full of promise and the closed stone space is really a tunnel out of misery, a hallway opening onto many rooms, a door to someplace remarkable we have not yet been. Solid things lose their substance in the light of Easter morning. For what was once an end is now a glorious beginning.

The Second Glorious Mystery

The Ascension

After his suffering, Jesus presented himself alive to them by many convincing proofs, appearing to them during forty days and speaking about the kingdom of God. During this time they asked him, "Lord, is this the time when you will restore the kingdom to Israel?" He replied, "It is not for you to know the times or periods that the Father has set by his own authority. But you will receive power when the Holy Spirit has come upon you, and you will be my witnesses in Jerusalem, in all Judea and Samaria, and to the ends of the earth."

When he had said this, as they were watching he was lifted up and a cloud took him out of their sight. While he was going and they were gazing up toward heaven, suddenly two men in white robes stood by them. They said, "Men of Galilee, why are you standing around looking up toward heaven? This Jesus, who has been taken up from you into heaven, will come in the same way as you saw him go."

—the Acts of the Apostles

Wonder is still available to us whenever we take the time to look up. Sunrise and sunset draw us with their unrivaled beauty. Star-gorgeous evenings compel us to gasp at the clarity and busy commerce of the heavens. Space is still "the final frontier." And no matter how many probes and persons ascend to those regions beyond our immediate vision, the reports that return to us seem nothing short of miraculous. Even a lazy sky full of cumulus clouds can capture our imagination and lure us into daydreams. A gleaming modern skyline may cause us to catch our breath as much as the jagged edge of mountains on the horizon.

But forces inhabit the skies that are less poetic. Long-ago meteors have crashed into the atmosphere, sending up clouds of debris that threatened the viability of our little planet, and other meteors could do so again. A hole in the protective layer of ozone may change our environment for generations to come. Weapons of mass destruction are pointed toward the skies in many lands, ready to be launched on command. Even the air itself is not as pure as it once was, and some regions are already experiencing an increase in childhood asthma, bronchial infections and cancers as a result of our careless exploitation of the environment.

Looking up at the sky is an invitation to awe or to trepidation—and sometimes to both at once. It was the same way for the ancients, who looked to the heavens and the gods that ruled them with a mixture of reverence and dread. The quaint phrase "fear of the Lord" was not simply a summons to respect. Not so many centuries ago, wariness—rather than love—seemed an appropriate response to the Almighty.

***

Third-millennium Christians look "up," metaphorically if not literally, with mixed feelings. Will there be a final, cataclysmic end to this world, and what if anything will follow? Will such an end come in the far distant future, after our great star burns out and the solar system cools, or will a single act of human lunacy lead to our destruction? Will we as a race ruin our planet's viability by neglect or greed or a long chain of foolish decisions? Will God, with a wave of the divine hand, set into motion the Apocalypse, with its avenging angels, fearsome horsemen, pestilence and monstrous personalities of evil?

The Catholic understanding of "the last things" does not square with biblical fundamentalism in this regard. The Church does not teach that God has a specific plan to eliminate creation, much less one outlined with such precision as found in the imagery of the Book of Revelation. Contained within "the last things," as Catholic scholars read this book, is the assurance that God will prevail, despite whatever horror descends upon the earth. Although evil seems to rule for a time, the victory is in heaven's hands all the while. We are not granted a blow-by-blow scenario for how things will end, but we are given absolute confidence that God is the ultimate authority over the living and the dead. Eternal joy is never in doubt for those who believe that.

***

Scripture speaks of "a new heavens and a new earth, where the justice of God will reign" (2 Peter 3:13). It would seem that the restoration of creation to its original goodness is more in keeping with God's desire than a scenario of mass destruction. But God does not promote a divine design over the primacy of human free will. Thus if we choose to foster injustice with our greed and fan the flames of chaos in our love affair with power, then we will surely reap the bitterness we sow. God will not save us from ourselves. But God does save us from our sins. We merely decide whether or not salvation is something that motivates us.

***

Jesus calls his disciples to follow him. The last reported Jesus sighting in the Acts of the Apostles is of him returning to his Father in the most unconventional way imaginable in his Ascension. Are we to follow Jesus in that precise way? The angels who appear immediately on the scene discourage the kind of thinking that idealizes a snatched-up-to-heaven approach as described in pop literature about the "Rapture." The disciples are told to focus not on Jesus' miraculous departure but on his certain and provocative return. That "hour" merits our attention as well.

As Saint Bernard of Clairvaux described it, Jesus' Second Coming is one of three "comings" of Jesus that should seriously concern us. Jesus came first in the Incarnation, revealing God's desire to meet us in the flesh and bring us closer to the divine. Christ will return at the close of history, ushering in a reign of God that will have no end. That time is also an hour of judgment for the living and the dead. But the most significant coming of Jesus, in Bernard's way of thinking, is the constant arrival of Jesus in every hour. It is here we meet our Lord and serve him. Only in the holy and vital present hour can we define our response to his gospel and influence our last encounter with him in the final judgment. "Now is the time; today is the day of our salvation," as Paul wrote in 2 Corinthians 6:2. We cannot hope to find salvation on the last day if we have not chosen it on *this* day.

The virtue of hope, to which this mystery of the rosary points, is not about wishfully thinking but deliberately choosing. Hope is ours not by daydreaming about it but by putting our faith into action. For this we do not have to look up into the heavens. We can find what we seek in the faces of our sisters and brothers.

The Third Glorious Mystery

The Descent of the Holy Spirit

When the day of Pentecost had come, they were all together in one place. Suddenly from heaven came a sound like the rush of a violent wind, which filled the house where they were sitting. Divided tongues as of fire appeared among them, and a tongue rested on each of them. All were filled with the Holy Spirit and began to speak in other languages, as the Spirit gave them ability.

Now there were devout Jews from every nation under heaven living in Jerusalem. And at this sound the crowd gathered and was bewildered, because each one heard the disciples speaking in their native language. Amazed and astonished, they asked, "Are not all these who are speaking Galileans? And how is it that we hear, each of us, in our own native tongue?" All were amazed and perplexed, saying to one another, "What does this mean?"

—the Acts of the Apostles

Charismatic Catholics and Pentecostal Protestants will be the first to tell us that the Holy Spirit is where the action is for disciples of Jesus. The Holy Spirit is where the rubber meets the road in Christianity. The stories of Hebrew Scripture are important for understanding the history of God's people; the Gospels are crucial in accepting the lordship of Jesus Christ; and the Church can teach us its tradition and nurture us with its sacraments. But without the power of the Holy Spirit, all we have is the thin broth of religion with no substance.

Jesus, in fact, never envisioned the Church without this central and emanating force. At the Last Supper he assured his disciples that even as he left them he was preparing to send his Spirit to lead and empower them. The two movements were of such a piece that it was vital for Jesus to leave so that the Spirit could be sent. As Jesus lived among them, he had brought his friends along with teachings, signs and wonders. But the Spirit would do things beyond his leadership, for it would dwell within the disciples and make them leaders in their own right.

The Acts of the Apostles is a fascinating church document, for it tells the startling story of what that indwelling Spirit would do with this little band that once cowered in fear before the powers of Jerusalem and Rome. These timid folk would become giants of the faith, whose names would be hallowed and mounted on churches. Their creed would be passed down for centuries, and their example of martyrdom would lead untold numbers to lay down their lives with the same bold testimony.

***

What incredible force does this Spirit possess to so transform weak human hearts? Saint Paul, the analyst and spiritual chemist, was the first to try to break down the Spirit's action into its component parts. He quoted the prophet Isaiah's list of divine gifts as originating in the reception of the Spirit (see Isaiah 11:2–3): wisdom, understanding, knowledge, counsel, courage, reverence and awe in the presence of God. These are the gifts associated with the sacrament of confirmation. Paul also observed how a person's life would become fruitful in the Spirit, bearing the telltale signs of love, joy, peace, patience, kindness, generosity, faithfulness, gentleness and self-control (see Galatians 5:22–23). If you saw a person exhibiting these magnificent graces, you were witnessing the work of the Spirit alive in him or her.

But Paul also told us that Christian vocation springs from this same Spirit (see 1 Corinthians 12:3b–28). Those who teach, preach, give prophetic witness, spread the faith, or offer healing, service or leadership all act under the Spirit's sway. So do those who "speak in tongues," a peculiar inspired speech that accompanies deep prayer influenced by the Spirit's power. Paul cautioned his communities, however, not to seek this last gift for its own sake. The power of inspired speech too often led those who expressed it to feel superior to those who did not have it.

Paul gave the Church its first theology of the Holy Spirit, and it remains the clearest path to discerning the Spirit's activity today. But talk is cheap, as Paul might have said. What is more urgent is to cooperate personally with the Spirit's movement at every opportunity.

***

Many traditional Catholics may feel a certain anxiety about close encounters with the Third Person of the Trinity. Some of us have relegated the Spirit to the confines of early church history, a special period of grace that came to an end with the death of the original apostles. We certainly understand that the gifts of tongues and other supernatural powers belong in the Bible, but we wonder whether there is room for them in the modern world of economic decision-making and keeping families together.

It may serve us well to revisit the first Pentecost and examine what the gift of inspired language was principally for. Far from the unintelligible speech of later charismatic communities, the language that descended upon the first disciples was miraculously comprehensible. Rather than being a secret and mysterious language, the tongues of Pentecost led to words remarkable for their very accessibility. It was the reversal of the curse of Babel, the ancient tower to heaven that brought the garbling of human language to the earth to begin with. Suddenly, far from being separated by nation, race and tongue, people were drawn together by holy speech that everyone could clearly understand.

Would that this language was spoken into our world today. Would that someone still possessed the gift to speak "in the language of angels" that would resound with the same meaning for all women and men, regardless of their nationality. Modern diplomats, influenced by their individual nation's policies and self-interest, hardly dare to speak the language that preserves and benefits all. Contemporary religious leaders look to their own creeds, and no one seems to have the courage to pronounce a word that can cross borders and be readily understood to offer mutual encouragement and hope.

***

But the unifying language of the Holy Spirit is not lost to today's world. Nor are the other gifts of the Spirit on historical hold. Those who would experience the indwelling Spirit once again have only to ask for it. Every sacrament of the Church is a confirmation of the Spirit's life at work within us. If we do not know this power for ourselves, it does not mean we do not carry it. As Catholics used to say, we are temples of the Holy Spirit, each of us lamps bearing the light of the world, which must not be hidden.

We can take another lesson from Mary, the original temple in whom the Spirit lived most dynamically and who brought forth Christ so literally: The power of God yearns to be expressed through us, but it will do nothing without our consent. If we want to participate in the expression of divine will in our own times, all we have to do is say, as Mary said, "Let it be done." God will do it, and perhaps the language of angels will be spoken in our world once more.

The Fourth Glorious Mystery

The Assumption of Mary

In heaven, God's temple was opened, and the ark of the covenant could be seen in it. A great sign appeared in the sky, a woman clothed with the sun, with the moon at her feet, wearing a crown of twelve stars. She was with child and wailed aloud in the pains of birth. Then another sign appeared: a huge red dragon with seven heads and ten horns, and on its heads were seven diadems. Its tail swept a third of the stars from the sky and hurled them to earth. The dragon stood before the woman, prepared to devour her child when she gave birth. She bore a son, destined to rule the nations with an iron rod. Her child was caught up to God. The woman herself fled into the desert, where God had prepared a place for her.

—the Book of Revelation

One of the most immediate encounters of our humanity is our bodily-ness. Being human means living in the flesh, and whatever that experience may be in a given moment, it is an inescapable part of our reality. Our physical appearance may seem comely or unruly to us. Our senses may communicate the robust pleasure of a summer morning or the bleak chill of a dark winter day. Our bodies may be youthful, lithe and agile, or we may be subject to the daily weakness and pain of failing health. The instinct of attraction, the ache of desire and loneliness, the comfort of companionship—all of this and more is knit into our flesh. Although we may try to spiritualize them out of our consciousness, our bodies are here to stay for as long as we are.

The delights of the senses are many: the beauty of a flowering tree in the spring, the sensuality of velvet, Beethoven's *Ode to Joy,* delicious holiday food, the sharing of our story with another soul. But we also know that flesh-and-blood is a precarious state to be in. Things go wrong with our bodies that make our experience of them a double-edged sword. How many of us have watched the silent burden of a diabetic friend taking his needle-stick with patience and resignation. How many of us have shuddered at the misery of a sister undergoing chemotherapy or dialysis. How many of us have felt the shock of physical violence, the trauma of sexual assault, the horrors of war, the fear of encroaching disability? Being made of flesh and blood makes us vulnerable to "the heartache and the thousand natural shocks that flesh is heir to," as Hamlet once mourned. Scripture reminds us that "flesh is grass" as we trace the mortal arc from birth to ashes (see Isaiah 40:6–8). We may have come from dust, but we resist our return there with all our might.

***

The story of Mary's Assumption is a divinely inspired response to our deepest fears as well as our greatest hopes about the fate of our bodies. Although the dogma was not pronounced until 1950, the Assumption has been celebrated by the Church since the sixth century.

The death of Mary is not recorded in Scripture, which means this mystery has a different sort of "biblical imprint" than most others in the rosary. Rather than looking to the report of a particular event, we look to the great themes and values of salvation history. On the Feast of the Assumption, the Church reflects on stories about the Ark of the Covenant, that physical place in which the presence of God chose to dwell in ancient Israel. Early church writers understood that Mary of Nazareth became the ark of our salvation in a new and spectacular way in the New Testament, bearing the God-Made-Flesh within her womb. God chose to live among us in a new way in the body of this woman. Her very being was infused with this unique and privileged role. Human flesh was never so ennobled as when God chose to reside within it.

The other teaching about Mary, the Immaculate Conception, is intimately linked with the Assumption. If Mary is understood to be the ark of God's presence, then her body is a holy vessel to be preserved from sin (immaculate) and its effect (the corruption of death). Mary does not lose her humanity in all this. The dignity of all humanity is elevated by her special participation in salvation history. Mary, the Mother of the Church, is the realization of the destiny of the whole Church. Just as she was protected, preserved and lifted up, so we anticipate we will be as well.

***

The timing of the promulgation of the dogma of the Assumption was no accident of history. After half a century of some of the most brutal wars of modern times, the Church chose to underscore its teaching about the dignity of the human person—body and soul—before God. We think of the Assumption as a teaching about Mary, but it also affirms the significance of the creatureliness of all humans before the Maker of all. After the horrors and humiliations visited upon human bodies in the battlefields and gas chambers of World War II, it was poignant to consider how God sees and values the human person. If every hair on our head is counted by our Creator, then every hair that falls in old age or through radiation treatments also is counted. When we contemplate the image in Revelation of the woman who is protected and provided for by the hand of God, we see not only the final safety (salvation) we know as Christians but also the real care and closeness of God throughout our encounters with the red dragons of this world. Although the wheels of history and human choices may crush us, although national or personal tragedy may overcome us, God is near and *we will be lifted up.* The image of Mary's Assumption assures us of this.

***

In our own time, the human body is hardly free from assault. We are in danger of becoming psychologically immune to the number of bombs dropped on enemies and innocents alike in every conflict. The trivialization of sexuality degrades and demoralizes us, especially the young, as they wonder where to seek genuine intimacy that is not often reflected in the culture around them. We grow numb in the face of statistics about AIDS and cancer. We mourn the tragic loss of life through abortion. We become accustomed to our instinct for vengeance in capital punishment. We regret the isolation of the elderly who suffer untold indignities in clinical settings far removed from home. Just as tradition teaches that Mary was lifted up body and soul to live with the God who once lived in her, so we lift up our prayer that the dignity and holiness of the whole human person may be restored, flesh and spirit together.

The Fifth Glorious Mystery

The Crowning of Mary

> The queen stands at the right hand of the king,
> arrayed in the gold of Ophir.
> Hear, my daughter, and understand;
> listen to the sound of my voice.
> Forget your people and your family home:
> the king desires your beauty.
> Honor your lord, and the rich will seek
> your favor with gifts.
> All glorious is she as she enters,
> her raiment threaded with gold.
> She is accompanied with gladness and joy
> as her companions enter the palace of the king.
> —*Psalm 45*

Those who grew up Catholic and attended parochial schools may remember the May crownings that were celebrated as naturally as spring followed winter. The first flowers of the season wound up at the feet of the Madonna, and some were woven into a wreath for her veiled hair. A young girl would be favored to place that crown on the Virgin's head, while the rest sang songs reaching back to antiquity—or at least to Latin: *Salve Regina. Ave Maria. Ora, ora pro nobis.*

Back then, many Catholics of European descent had shrines dedicated to Mary in their homes or gardens, honoring her familiar image in the Immaculate Heart, the Madonna and Child, Our Lady of Lourdes or Our Lady of Fatima. Honoring the Blessed Mother was a reflexive part of being Catholic. A generation ago, the average Catholic was less aware or concerned about theology than today. No one worried that the coronation of Mary was not mentioned in the Bible. She was Queen of Heaven in our hearts.

Psychologist Carl Jung, decidedly not a Catholic, admired the Church's tenacity in keeping the Mother of God just off to one side of the Trinity in its devotional world. Jung saw the Catholic devotion to Mary as a restoration of the balance of the feminine in an otherwise male-dominated Godhead. Feminists would later see in Mary a way that medieval folk kept close at hand the ancient devotion to the goddess. Meanwhile, we can imagine Mary our Mother receiving our theology and psychology and politics about her as graciously as when we placed that wreath of flowers on her head.

Still, the question must be asked: In what sense is our talk about the queenship of Mary "real"?

***

Talk of celestial realities is evident throughout the Bible, although it is written in terms of *revelation*, a lifting of the veil that separates God's perspective from ours. When we begin to extract from the text the literal trumpet-blowing angels and heavenly horsemen, however, assigning them with specific values according to our own times, we run into trouble. The queenship of Mary, like the kingship of Christ, can lead us to similar confusion if we embrace these images in terms of modern monarchy. In royal-phobic America, who needs a king and queen? What do these ancient symbols have to offer in the land of democratic election and republican representation?

Mary was named Queen of Heaven as an honorific title, equivalent to the names Our Lady and Our Blessed Mother. Elizabeth intended a similar honor when she saw her young cousin miraculously with child and called her "Mother of my Lord" (Luke 1:43). Mary's queenship is closely tied to her role as Mother of God and Mother of the Faithful. To understand this, consider how ancient kings were chosen by prophetically inspired anointing, each becoming *messiah*, "anointed one," for his people. This divinely recognized right to rule included by extension the whole royal house. Royal folk had no mere temporal power but rather wielded the authority given by God. If they should lose God's favor—and many did—their authority crumbled into nothing.

Mary, chosen by God for the task of bringing forth the Alpha and the Omega of all messiahs, by extension becomes part of a royal household. Her maternal queenship is not temporal, just as Jesus wielded no secular authority and held no public office. Yet she who was once the humble handmaid of the Lord would become the Queen of Mercy and the Mother of Grace for the whole Church. This is why Pope John Paul II has written that "the Marian dimension of the church precedes the Petrine" (see the *Catechism of the Catholic Church,* no. 773). This means that Mary, in a sense, comes *before* Peter. Mary Queen of Heaven has more authority than the pope sitting in Peter's chair on earth. (This thought may give courage to Catholic women everywhere who feel that their contributions to the Church have not been sufficiently recognized.)

***

We have considered what the queenship of Mary means for her, but what does it mean for us? As pre-eminent member and symbol of the Church, Mary's royal status reminds us that we too are a "holy nation, a royal priesthood," called to live in the reign of God as heirs of the kingdom that has no end. (1 Peter 2:9) What Mary already possesses in the City of God is the vision of what awaits us as her children in faith. That is why the traditional fruit assigned to praying this mystery of the rosary is eternal happiness. We acknowledge Mary's stature among the saints as a foreshadowing of the place God has prepared for those who likewise "believe that the Lord's word will be fulfilled" for us (Luke 1:45).

Our celebration of Mary's queenship, then, is a celebration of our membership in the royal family of Christ. Today we incorporate more diverse images of Mary—the pregnant Mestizo presence of Our Lady of Guadalupe, African and Asian Madonnas, the vulnerably young Madonna of the Streets. We find new ways to honor the woman who stands behind all these images at the center of salvation history.

In the story of Guadalupe, Our Lady reassured the faltering Juan Diego: "Do not be afraid. You have nothing to fear. Am I not here, your compassionate mother?" And so she was: appearing as a woman who was part Native American and part European, rejecting none of her children, even when they are in conflict with one another.

Mary's willingness to be Mother of Us All remains at the heart of her queenship. Whether we choose to "crown her with blossoms today" as the old hymn says or simply embrace her intercession and protection, it is she who does us the honor of being our "holy Queen," our "Mother of mercy."

Epilogue

The Rosary for a Third-Millennium Church

For quite some time, the rosary has been viewed as a staid and traditional prayer that is the exclusive domain of traditional Catholics, although the new Mysteries of Light have caused many to take a fresh look at it. It may seem odd to suggest that it might become a tool for a new revolution or that we might discover the practice of praying the rosary to be radically countercultural. But I believe that the rosary has within itself the potential to change hearts and—in the very act of doing so—to change the world.

Pope John Paul II has asserted that the rosary is by its nature a prayer for peace because it hinges on Christ, who is our peace, as Saint Paul reminds us in the Letter to the Ephesians. But more than that, the rosary contemplates "a life of humility, poverty, hiddenness, patience and perfection" (*Rosarium Virginis Mariae*, no. 16), which is precisely the opposite direction worldly values are taking us. The spirit of these twenty mysteries, when deeply incorporated, cannot embrace the aggression, self-absorption and greed that characterize much of our third millennium. A "rosary personality" would stand as a witness against violence, injustice, intolerance, ecological outrage and superpower self-aggrandizement. It is not impossible to think that one day rosary-bearing Catholics, liberals and conservatives alike, might wind up in the town square, in Washington, or at the United Nations, protesting or supporting actions for or against the Christian conscience in the full spectrum of issues that oppress and violate the great gift of life.

Our age is one of image making, and through the media we are continually assaulted with images of destruction and malice, war and death, greed and waste. The rosary invites us to contemplate very different images of salvation and sanctification, of blessing and boundless compassion. If we gave ourselves over to such prayer with a fraction of the time we spend watching television, the pope suggests, we might be surprised at how the rosary's much more peace-promoting images could inform and reform us. In turning our eyes toward Jesus and Mary, we would simultaneously "regain the ability to look one another in the eye" (*Rosarium Virginis Mariae,* no. 41) This renewed sense of vision also enables us to face the problems of our times with "responsible and generous eyes" (no. 40) Do we retain enough hope in our hearts to trust in such a personal transfiguration?

In the end, the Catholic stance is best known in confiding oneself to the notion of *mystery,* which surpasses all information and rational understanding. The revelation of Jesus is utter mystery: how divinity becomes humanity, eternity enters flesh, God's Son is put to death, and death is repealed in the Resurrection to new life. The mystery of Christ is the great illuminator of the mystery implicit in the sacred quality of mortal life: how our salvation is knit to our suffering and how we each have a unique and necessary role to play in the unfolding of creation.

The rosary is one way of contemplating and assimilating this mystery. Its repetitions bear the mark of the dynamic of human love, which cannot be contemplated too often without taking shape, sometimes quite literally, in the flesh. Jesus asked Simon Peter three times to declare his love. We can imagine that it did as much good for Peter to say it out loud three times as it did for the Lord to hear it. The words of love have not been heard so often in our world that they do not bear repeating. Their incarnation in our lives would surely be, in this and every age, a revolution to behold.